Rethinking Hope

Rethinking Hope

Christian Eschatology Rediscovered

K. A. Abraham

Christian World Imprints

First Published in 2021 by

Christian World Imprints
Christian Publishing & Books from India
C-3, Wazirpur Industrial Area
Delhi-110052
cwidelhi2017@gmail.com
www.ChristianWorldImprints.com
Phone: +91 11 41526079

ISBN: 978-93-5148-511-7 (HB)
ISBN: 978-93-5148-512-4 (PB)

Printed in India.

Contents

Foreword:
Dr. Theodosius Mar Thoma Metropolitan

"Rethinking Hope: Christian Eschatology Rediscovered" is a new book written by Rev. Dr. K. A. Abraham who has given me the privilege to write a foreword. This is a scholarly work by him in an area that people seldom dare to write at length. Rev. Dr. K. A. Abraham has a long teaching experience in the Mar Thoma Theological Seminary, Kottayam and The Federated Faculty For Research In Religion & Culture (FFRRC) of Serampore University in Kottayam, Kerala. He was a Parish priest in various parishes of the Malankara Mar Thoma Syrian Church in India and abroad. He was often invited by various Churches and Christian centers for teaching ministry in Christian Doctrines. The invitation he got to travel the length and breadth of North America in 1999 to take classes for the members of the Church gave him an opportunity to prepare 'Eschatology and the Second coming of Christ.' This paved the way for him to prepare this book.

The book finds its shape from the author's academic pursuit and the long Pastoral vocation. The perspective of this book is mainly theological as the author himself is a research scholar in systematic theology. The book reveals how the author scholarly analyses the theme by going through the various related topics through the 14 chapters of the book before he draws his conclusion. The readers will enjoy how the author is highlighting the essential topics in relation to the contemporary scenario of our lives with a proposal for the furtherance of our faith.

Eschatology is a doctrine where all the members of the Church generally fail to understand because they are pulled to different doctrines by both evangelicals and radicals who also are often confused on the basic tenets of Christianity. The Eschatological is not just one element of Christianity, but it is the medium of Christian faith as such. Christianity is a forward looking and forward moving community that lives in hope for revolutionizing and transforming the present world. This redemptive approach guided by the Holy Spirit to make all things new, has a creative expectancy that is based on the cross and redemption of Jesus Christ. This approach negates all sorts of fatalism and determinism in all fields.

I am writing this at a time where the whole world is in a flux due to the attack of the invisible Corona Virus. There is a wide spread fear and anxiety everywhere. Thousands of people are losing their precious lives. Medical field is going through new experiences as there is no vaccine till date to prevent the epidemic. There are larger number of people who are subject to quarantine. The daily wage labourers have no work, no money and no food. They migrate from their place of work to their native place in spite of the difficulties they have to encounter on travel. Wearing masks, using sanitizers and keeping physical distance in social circles are all bringing new lifestyle to the people. There are a good number of people asking the question, 'Is this the end of time?' The task of the historians is to make sense of the historical events. This book is becoming very relevant as the author is responding to Covid-19 at several sections of the book. The book asserts that 'hope' is God's doing within humans and the human task is to discern God's work in the world. This is also a call for us to be the agents of hope at all levels. The challenge is to understand Christian spirituality, not in the individual dimension but in relationship with God, with other human beings and with nature. Therefore, hope is a shared hope. The present Covid-19 pandemic is reassuring us that God's empowering presence is in the world and with the people. As humans we are invited to turn to God as God has already turned to us through Jesus Christ who is our eternal contemporary. God instills rays of hope in the midst of despair and hopelessness. God is always active in his creation. He grants us hope always and this hope is for the entire world.

Studying the topic of eschatology requires that one look into the topic of the Second coming of Christ, the day of the Lord, Rapture, consummation in the Kingdom of God, Final Judgement, the End, the Death, New Heaven and New Earth, Eternal life and the like. The author is making a detailed study in all these topics and with much clarity in pointing out that the church, the community of communities, has a very significant role to be a community of hope, promoting hope at different levels. What the church needs today is a fresh search for meaning and clarity on the mystery of life in the context of the present historical ambiguities & predicaments.

What makes our 'Life of Faith' authentic? Christian faith has both historical as well as trans-historical dimensions. When both the Jewish and Christian doctrines of eschatology emphasize the dawn of a 'new age', the task of the church is to 'see beyond' and to 'reach out in hope.' Life is not always solving problems; sometimes it will be coping with them and leave the outcome confidently and with hope in the hands of God. When we realize that the anchor of the Christian hope is Jesus Christ, his cross and resurrection, He challenges us to face the harsh realities of life confidently, leaving the withdrawal tendency and also the spirit of escapism. The eschatology that we hold on to is down to earth, doctrine like the cross of Christ, an eschatology that would empower us in our faith journey. Therefore, eschatology is not a 'wishful thinking or facile optimism but an active hope which begins and grows in our concrete life, right here on earth and culminates in the fullness of eternity.

Rev. Dr. K. A. Abraham is looking up into the various faith traditions of the Christian denominations and brings in illustrations mostly from his own faith tradition. He is looking into the W.C.C. Theme of various General Assemblies and brings in relevant reflection on the topic of his book. As an Indian, he is also making use of various Indian traditions and reflects on the contributions of Indian Christian Theologians.

This theological treatise is an asset and a great text for all students, clergy and all research scholars who want a balanced meaningful doctrine on Christian Hope. As the title says, Dr. Abraham has rediscovered Christian Eschatology and is now challenging every reader to re-think one's concept of the doctrine of 'Hope.' I do not think that there is another book on the topic by another Indian author. At the same time, the present author is not claiming that the book is a final word on the topic. This book should inspire a greater number of budding scholars to criticize the content and research more for newer publications. With great appreciation to the author who labored hard and researched extensively on available materials, I happily present this book before the wider public for an in-depth study and serious criticism. I am certain that this book will be a blessing to a number of people in different walks of life. I wish the publication of this book all success and all the readers a blessed learning.

Dr. Theodosius Mar Thoma
Metropolitan, Mar Thoma Poolatheen
Thiruvalla

Acknowledgements

My special interest in the area of Eschatology goes back to 1999 when The Late Dr. Zacharias Mar Theophiplus Saffragon Metropolitan invited me for a series of study sessions on the topic, “Eschatology & the Second Coming of Christ” in the Mar Thoma Diocese of North America and Europe. These were study conventions of the Diocese in different centers; New York, Philadelphia, Dallas, Chicago and Houston. In some places there were open forums after each session. In spite of my attempt to make the sessions as communicative as possible; as usual, among the audience some were receptive and some others found their inherited theology and Bible knowledge challenged! The insights given in the book are the elaborated version of these talks. I am indebted to Late Bishop Mar Theophilos for this opportunity and also for the encouragement in my academic and pastoral vocation. Ever since these events, I deliberately made it a topic in the Parish ministry in the Mar Thoma Church at different places. Recently in the Silicon valley Mar Thoma Church, San Francisco, U.S, a few sessions were taken on the topic “Dimensions of Christian Eschatology” which led to discussion at different levels.

I thank God the Almighty for calling me to be in His ministry and for the providence for the last forty years in my academic and pastoral vocation, and especially for enabling me to publish this book. My special gratitude to Dr. Theodosius Mar Thoma Metropolitan for his graceful, profound and in-depth words in the Foreword. I am grateful to Rev. Larry Philip Varghese, my former student at the Mar Thoma Theological Seminary and my son-in-Law, for meticulously reviewing my manuscript and making editorial corrections where ever necessary. Last but not the least, my special thanks to Annis Abraham, my wife, who always stood with me in my academic and pastoral vocation and our children, Roshin and Christy and their families for continuously reminding me that academic exploration should not be at the expense of family commitments. I am also thankful to Christian World Imprints, New Delhi for publishing this book.

Rev. Dr. K. A. Abraham

1

Introduction

Eschatology is a topic that is very often seen with enthusiasm in certain evangelical spiritual circles and similarly suspicion in theologically radical circles. In the Seminary syllabus, this is always taught towards the end. It seems that both the evangelicals and radicals fail to comprehend the basic tenets of the doctrine of Eschatology. In the contemporary "New Generation" churches and spiritual circles, this is taught as if it has nothing to do with our earthly life and its realities. There is so much of world negation and statusquo tendencies here. It is as if God decides everything and human involvement in history is of no use. There is a dominant thinking in our church traditions that this worldly life is only a preparatory ground for the eternal life which is after death. Similarly, in contemporary theology this topic is almost ignored. This is due to our thinking that Eschatology has to do with our ultimate future. Nevertheless, a few books in this area deserve special mention. They are: *The Coming of God* by Jurgen Moltmann, *Surprised by Hope* and *History and Eschatology*, both by Bishop N. T. Wright and *The Rapture Exposed* by Barbara R. Rossing.

The author has always been of the view that there should not be a dichotomy between academic excellence and pastoral vocation. As the Patristic fathers have pointed out, faith here is intellectual illumination.

What is Eschatology?

Eschatos in Greek has to do with the study of last things, end times, the ultimate destiny of humankind and the whole cosmos etc. Some of the frequently asked questions here are the following:

What is the ultimate meaning of life on earth?
Does this world have a future?

Does human life have a divine purpose?
What is the historical function and role of the Church?
Does God allow sin and evil to flourish?
Is there a final victory of God over the forces of evil?

In our attempt to answer some of the above questions, both a negation of this world and glorification of this world are to be avoided. There have been attempts in history and in the tradition of the church to give answers to some of these questions.

Well, why this book?

A story is told about Hugo Gryn, a Jewish Rabbi who was in the Nazi concentration camp in Germany. With the oil that was served as part of the daily ration, he tried to light a Hanukah Lamp. His son was surprised at this and asked "Dad, why this lamp in the concentration camp?" He replied, "You can live three weeks without food; three days without water; but you cannot live properly three minutes without hope."

This book comes out of the author's academic pursuit and long pastoral vocation. The author has a feeling that the theme of Eschatology is mostly preached or studied in Pentecost, Brethren and New Generation churches. This is mostly done without due attention to the historical context of the Biblical narratives and also in a world negation notion. The so-called Bible-belt churches in U.S are always for the promotion of wars by quoting mainly from the eschatological passages in the book of Daniel and Revelation. But, very little significance is given to this theme in the main line churches. Nevertheless, I deliberately made it a topic in the parish ministry.

Since the author's field of study and research is Systematic Theology, the perspective of the book is mainly theological. Nevertheless, insights from Biblical and sociological scholarship are used wherever necessary. The author doesn't claim to make a final word on the topic. Some of the insights may be problematic and controversial. The author has in mind the clergy across church traditions, theological students, Sunday School teachers and lay leaders among the readership of the book. Your comments and critiques are most welcome.

To begin with, a survey of a few secular and religious eschatologies is essential. For example, in Marxian ideology there is the concept of the "progressive perfection of history." What matters here is human involvement in historical events, struggle for a just society, fight for human rights etc. However, God is not acknowledged here. It is as if this history is self-redemptive which is not an acceptable notion in Christian theology. This is not to underestimate the role of secular ideologies in the transformation of history. In Kerala for example, two significant movements in the transformation of society are the Missionary Movement and the Communist movement.

The bold stances of scholars and visionaries like Swami Agnivesh, Swami Sandeepanada Giri, Prof. Sunil P. Elayidam are definitely the secular versions of hope in our times. For example, Swami Sandeepanda Giri points out that there is a clear distinction between Hindutva and the Hindu dharma as the former is a political project with communal and opportunistic interests and the latter is a *darsana* (vision) with an inclusive vision. Similarly, Sunil P. Elayidam who is in the forefront of the struggle against the discriminatory Citizenship Amendment Bill, points out that religion is not to be seen as ritual but as value. All these scholars and several others in different religious traditions and a few Marxists are unequivocally supporting the cause of the weak and marginalized and some of them are paying a heavy price for their positions. Several of them were brutally attacked by the Hindutva fundamentalists, the so-called guardians of Indian culture! On the whole, these stances are for an ideal, egalitarian state of affairs, a situation of wellness for all, promotion of values such as freedom, equality, justice etc.

In Hinduism there are four *yugas* (aeons): krita, treata, dwapara, and kali. The traditional understanding is that this is kali yuga and during this period, evil has the upper hand. Nevertheless, there have been attempts to reinterpret this by Neo-Hindus mainly because of the element of fatalism. The late M. M. Thomas finds a secular version of Christian hope even in the Onam myth in Kerala.

The so-called Western (Christian) view is the linear one. Here history is considered as a straight line. For example, "I am the alpha and the omega" (Rev. 1:8). But even Western scholars are critical of this position. They are of the view that history has never been like that; there has always been ups and downs in the development of history.

Even though the author is of the view that the main eschatological themes are the Kingdom of God, New Heaven and New Earth and so on, an attempt is made to include a chapter on "Millenarianism and Rapture" as it is considered by the end time enthusiasts as the most significant area of this theme. The examples and events in the text are mostly from the Indian context as the author believes that contextual reflections are inevitable in theological endeavour. Nevertheless, the global contexts are also given due attention. The book is neither a Bible study nor an academic treatise per se, even though Biblical and theological insights are included wherever necessary. The author doesn't claim any expertise in the area of Eschatology; the book may be treated a humble attempt to rediscover a theme in the light of some of the contemporary realities. The rationale for the book is that this topic is almost ignored in the main line churches and over emphasized in the Pentecost, New Generation traditions – that too in an allegoric, other worldly, and ahistorical way. Rather than being satisfied with some kind of a "feel good no matter what factor", that is very often found in Christian eschatology, the attempt here is to delve deep into the essence and different components of eschatology, with special reference to Christian hope. Some of the traditional, deterministic notions and myths are exploded in this task. On the whole, the intention of the author is a thematic, theological analysis of the theme.

Some of the end time enthusiasts may find some pages of this book disturbing. My request to them is to read the book carefully till the end without any value judgments. It is to be noted that the book attempts to develop a theme and only selective use and exposition of the Biblical texts are given in the book. The author doesn't claim that this is the final word on the theme; rather he is open to creative criticisms and suggestions. Rather than the projection of the theme of Eschatology, the basic concern is to highlight some of the essential themes and concerns for the furtherance of our life of faith. The topic of eschatology, with special reference to Christian hope is significant, more than ever before, in the context of the onslaught of COVID 19. The unprecedented corona pandemic, which has caused havoc across the world, has bewildered many, both in the religious and secular world. It's almost like a 'shaking of the foundations'! We have already had several responses such as: disciplinary evil, God's wrath for human sin, human alienation from nature and its equilibrium and as usual from the end time specialists, as the sign of the end times and so on. Rather than rational interpretations, the need of the times is to cope with the crisis, as our counselors very often point out. The last chapter of this book will specially deal with this crisis from a Christian theology perspective.

2

The Place of Eschatology in Christian Theology

The purpose of this chapter is to point out that Christian eschatology should be grounded in the Bible and rooted in history. So, any ahistorical approaches to eschatology are alien to the Biblical truth. What is to be underscored here is a "redemptive view of history." A brief survey of the different eschatological methods and Schools of thought are given to bring to the fore the scope of eschatology in our life of faith and also in the academic pursuit. The last section, the historical development of eschatology shows that the doctrine of eschatology has a history; and it's not an invention of the contemporary end time enthusiasts!

The early Christian eschatology was mainly individualistic. For example, life after death, last judgment, heaven and hell, and in the Roman Catholic circles, purgatory, etc., were the defining factors during this period. A wider concern in eschatology in terms of community and the whole creation is a later development. A purely futuristic and individualistic eschatology has been questioned by many. For example, C. H. Dodd talks about "a realistic eschatology" and R. H. Fuller, "an inaugurated eschatology." According to Fuller, John's Gospel emphasizes an inaugurated eschatology over against a futuristic one (Jn. 5:24; 12:31). In the Synoptic Gospels, we have the "already" (Kingdom of God is in your midst) and the "not yet" (Thy Kingdom come) of the Kingdom of God. In other words, both the present and futuristic eschatological dimensions are spoken of. Here the three historical actions of God are significant: Creation, Redemption, and Consummation; and all these are heavily interwoven. This means that human beings and the entire creation will find their completion in God. In the words of Carl E. Braten, the whole of Christian theology is penetrated by eschatology. According to Biblical scholars, the otherworldly eschatological traits of the Old Testament are due to Hellenistic influence on Judaism. For example, the apocalyptic eschatology flourished during the intertestamental period. Moltmann is of the view that eschatology is not just one element of Christian theology; an eschatological outlook is at the core of every Christian existence. He also finds an "eschatological renaissance" in theology in the 20th century. His words give us several crucial take-off points in the upcoming sections of this book:

> "*From first to last, and not merely in the epilogue, Christianity is eschatology, is hope, is forward looking and forward moving, and therefore also revolutionizing and transforming the present. The eschatological is not just one element of Christianity, but it is the medium of Christian faith as such, the key in which everything is set, and the glow that suffuses everything here in the dawn of an expected new day. For Christian faith lives in the raising of the crucified Christ, and strains after the promises of the universal future of Christ...Hence eschatology cannot really be only a part of the Christian doctrine. Rather the eschatological outlook is characteristic of all Christian proclamation, of every Christian existence and the whole Church. There is therefore only one real problem in Christian theology, which its own object forces upon it and which it in turn forces on mankind (sic.) and on human thought: the problem of future.*"[1]

In other words, as mentioned earlier, Christian faith is centered in hope, which is a creative expectancy that is based on the cross and resurrection of Christ.

Dermot A. Lane underlines the following as the Principles of eschatological narratives. They are:

One: Eschatological statements are a particular interpretation of the potential of human experience, human experience shaped by the Christian reality of God's grace and Christ's mission.

Two: The language of eschatology is metaphorical, symbolic, dialectical and analogical. More than affirmation, what we have here is, perhaps, negation, as we have it in Indian Philosophy-God is *neti, neti* (Not this not that). A similar attempt is the *Apophatic* theology in the Eastern Orthodox tradition. This is the manner of speaking about God in negative terms, over against the *cataphatic*, which is affirmative Theology. The concern here is to maintain an 'element of mystery' or the incomprehensibility of God.

Three: Eschatology in our times should give due attention to some of the critical voices like Marx, Nietzsche and a few others that eschatology is a distraction from the pressing problems of contemporary life.[2]

Along with the above, the question is whether we need to have some guidelines in the interpretation of the eschatological texts in the Bible. At the out set, what is of great importance is to underscore a world-view behind the Word of God.

Some of the guidelines are given below:

- The inner connection between Creation and the New Creation. The God of creation is the one who leads it to its fulfillment.
- Kairological approach; ie. History is moving towards its perfection. 'Kairos' has to do with God's decisive involvement in the world. Hence, we are neither spectators nor onlookers of historical events but active participants.
- Centrality of the Christ Event in the process of renewal of creation.
- The question is not how I can be saved and go to heaven; but rather, how can I be in the salvific mission of Christ.
- The work of the Holy Spirit who makes all things new. Our task is to be with the Holy Spirit in the process of renewal in the world.
- missio Dei; in the light of God's mission in the world.
- God's grace; Perfection is not our doing: rather it's our response to God's saving grace.
- Praxis oriented eschatology; or an eschatology that doesn't take seriously our responsibility for God's creation is defective.
- A redemptive approach towards this world. This is a negation of fatalism and determinism in all fields.

1. Eschatology and History

History is not merely a record of the past; it's both a record of events and their interpretation. A historian usually asks the following questions to a historical event: What happened? How did it happen? Why did it happen? What are the given interpretations? Who are the characters involved? One of the significant aspects here is that there is no value free history. If so, every history is in a way biased; it could be a colonial bias, ethnic bias, caste bias, gender bias or colour bias. Here the basic question is whether we can see history as a movement rather than something that happened in the past and also what is the perspective that one holds in doing history – the perspective of the dominant and their narratives or the marginal and their narratives from the fringes?

In his classical work *History and Eschatology*, Bishop N. T. Wright gives the following meanings to the term *history*. History is:

- Events of the past: accumulation of data, almost all unknown and unknowable and also the knowable past with evidences. Here what really happened regularly demands that we study the motives and the intentions of the characters involved. Several of these events don't have written evidences but the historian tries to find evidences through other sources such as archaeology, stories of the people, etc.
- The written account of past events. There is no neutral history. In a way all documents are biased. For example, the history written during

the period of monarchy may support the rule of Kings and the history written during the period of the feudal Lords may support them. Of course, there are exceptions. The task of the historian here is to filter through the data and interpret them. In other words, the task of the historian here is to make sense of the historical events. Here selection and arrangement of facts involve the interpretive judgment of the historian.

- The task of researching and writing about things that actually happened as opposed to producing fiction or fantasy.
- Discerning and displaying a pattern or principle–and hence, some meaning within the things that actually happened. In other words, the question why such a thing happened is significant here.
- Lastly, the term is used to denote a meaningful sequence of events, or that they have a 'goal' in view.[3]

All these are useful insights in the development of a realistic eschatology. Having said that, let me attempt a few approaches to history; both secular as well as religious. I will try to briefly define the concepts and at the end of each my critical evaluation of it.

a. Progressive Perfection of History

As pointed out earlier, this is mainly found in secular ideologies such as Marxism. Marx understood history as the realm of class wars between the bourgeois and proletariat and the end will be the withering away of the State and the dictatorship of the proletariat. This is known as the 'Marxian Utopia.' This method of classical Marxism was considered by many – especially the Latin American Liberation theologians like Leonardo Boff, Gutierez, Segundo, and several others as the appropriate method in theological reflections. Whereas in the Indian context, the Dalit thinkers like A. P. Nirmal, V. Devasahayam, and others are critical of this method. According to them, in the Indian context, what looms large is the 'caste factor' and not the 'class factor.'

b. Cyclical Understanding of History

As pointed out earlier, this method is found mainly in the Hindu tradition. There is an element of fatalism here. This method was used by Brahmanical Hinduism in its hegemonic efforts in India. In the Indian context, the Brahmanical culture is considered to be the dominant one and the tribal, dalit, sub-altern as the protest ones. The main attempt of the Hindutva in India is to glorify the dominant culture and to subjugate the smaller cultural traditions. Very subtle attempts are made in different areas such as the Indian Science Congress, Indian Council of Historical Review, School text book revisions etc. In the words of Dr. K. N. Panikkar and Romila Tapar, well known historians of ancient India, these are nothing but the "saffronisation of Indian history."

According to some of the Dalit thinkers, the weapons used by Brahmanical Hinduism are knowledge, rituals, and myths. Dalit Bandhu, and historian N. J. Jose's book in Malayalam, *Kerala Parasuraman Pulaya Shatru* sheds light on this. The myth is that Kerala, a state in South India was created by Parasuram by throwing an axe from a distance, one of the *avatars* of Vishnu, the God of creation in Hinduism. According to the myth, God gave the entire land to the Brahmins! But, as Jose the historian points out, the land belonged to the early Dravidas and the Dalits who were the original inhabitants of the land. This myth is ritualized and this is part of the Hindu *nam japa* (evening prayer). The attempt here is to legitimize a hegemonic attempt. Surprisingly, this is sung even in the victims families, the Dalits!

c. Teleological Understanding of History

Teleology is from the Greek word *telos* which is translated as purpose, end, etc. The emphasis here is that history is moving towards a purpose. In other words, there is a definite continuum, a foreordained particular goal in history. As pointed out in the introduction, the understanding of purpose varies in different religious traditions and secular ideologies. Mostly, it is considered as 'Eschatology in terms of the future.'

d. Kairological Understanding of History

There are two words in Greek for time: *chronos* and *kairos. Chronos* is the usual, biological time. Chronology is from this word. Whereas *kairos* is God's decisive time in history. This is used in the New Testament for several of the deeds of Jesus. For example, Jesus says, "The right time has come, the Kingdom of God is near; repent and believe in the Good News." (Mk. 1:15). Here the 'right time' is the *kairos* of God to act and also the time to turn to God in faith.

e. Redemptive Understanding of History

I am of the opinion that this should be a Christian understanding in our times. But, here again, a few notions are to be questioned:

- Judgmental approach. In the context of the Corona pandemic several videos and messages are coming out from Christian spiritual leaders. Some have special remedies for all human problems! Some others present Jesus as a panacea to all problems. I am reminded of an evangelistic campaign of a particular organization. In its effort to evangelize a town, they had put up different banners and posters with the caption: "Jesus is the answer." It was evening time and the school students were on their way back home. One naughty student took out his pen and wrote underneath: "But what is the question?" In other words, what is the question to which Jesus is the answer. This is nothing but the "Method of Correlation" suggested by Paul Tillich, the Systematic theologian who lived in U.S. in the last Century.

- Disciplinary evil. This theory says that God allows some evil so that the faithful may know his love and grace. This approach is found in Judaism and Christianity. According to this theory God is in absolute control but the believers have to undergo a quota of suffering so that they may be purified. This is the typical pastoral approach that is found in almost all Christian traditions. .

But the question is whether these approaches would comfort those who are suffering; for example, the victims of unjust systems or those who are in terminal illness. The main problem here is that the element of grace is absent in these systems. Hence, the rationale for the last one; the Redemptive method. This method affirms that history is not self-redemptive and it stands in need of a redeemer. No human beings and no situations are beyond redemption. This approach enables one to work with a positive mind in the midst of adversities of life. We can find several people all over the world working for others' health, freedom, liberation, identity and so on. The best example here is the scores of the Health Department workers across the world, fighting the pandemic COVID 19; some even at the risk of their own life.

Human beings are historical beings and human destiny is essentially a historical destiny. History is not merely a record of the past events or personalities. It is basically the realm of human actions and options. Our obedience to God as concrete historical human beings is at the core of Christian faith. So, what we need is a historically mediated eschatology; an eschatology that would enable us to take the historical events seriously, yet transcend them. As Samartha suggests: Mere history is not a matter of final significance. The real issue concerns the status of history itself, as the totality of events determined by human decisions.[4]

The task here is to live within history and at the same time to transcend history. We are not mere spectators of history but responsible human beings who have a bounden task to renew the course of history through genuine involvement.

A question that is very often asked is whether we can emphasize the historical dimension of eschatology in the Indian context where we have a cyclical view of history and also the concept of *maya* in the Hindu tradition. Some attempts have been made by Indian Christian theologians to reflect on this issue. Among them, the one given by P. D. Devanandan is significant here. Unlike the traditional Christian interpretation that *maya* is a negation of history, Devanandan brings out the insight that *maya* is not the negation of history in Neo-Hinduism. *Maya* is not considered to be an illusion. He tries to interpret *maya* as follows:

This is a world of *maya*; a world which is both real and unreal, conditioned by time and shot through with eternity, the scene of divine activity. But, here the *sat-asat* nature of world-life is not understood in terms of Ultimate reality but in terms of final purpose.[5]

The contribution of Devanandan is the reinterpretation of the concept of *maya* from the realm of being to that of will and of purpose. Hence, in our life of faith, which inevitably has a historical anchorage, we need to affirm those historical forces that are pro-life and to denounce those forces that are anti-life. What we need here is a realistic approach to historical realities and also a selective and critical cooperation with all genuine forces.

We should do away with two negative notions: First, progressive perfection of history; the view that history is self-redemptive through human struggles alone. And second, historical determinism; the tendency to justify all historical ambiguities and contradictions which will negate genuine human involvement for change and renewal. It should be affirmed that the Christian faith encourages, stimulates, and rectifies the historical process. The task is to discern as to what extent Jesus Christ is an illuminating force in the midst of historical predicaments and uncertainties.

2. Methods in Eschatology

Christian ethical thinkers have identified the following methods in Eschatological reflections.

a. Eschatological Extrapolation

This is mainly assessment of the future in the light of the known values. What we have here is an extrapolation of human experiences. The basic logic here is that God's nature in the Bible is eschatological in nature.

According to Hendric Berkhof, the future is an extrapolation of what has already been given in Christ and the Holy Spirit. He also finds a 'leap element' in eschatology, a leap into the unknown, into God's future for his creation. Christological and pneumatological elements are interrelated here. This is also an attempt to go beyond the mundane or direct experiences.

The basic question here is whether this is a Christian utopia or a facile optimism or futurology. Moltmann is critical of this method. In his words, "Extrapolation sees the future as an extrapolated and extended present and hence it kills the very future character of the future!" The question is whether we can expect the ultimate fulfilment from penultimate things.

b. Eschatological Transposition

This is Karl Rahner's concept. Rahner was the main theologian behind the Vatican II (1962-1965), the decisive Council which was a landmark in the history of the Roman Catholic Church. This is basically a transposition of the experience of salvation from the mode of the beginning into the mode of consummation. In other words, the concern here is a transition into a new quality. In this method, beginning and end are two 'modes of existence.' The basis of our eschatological future depends on our experiences of salvation here on earth.

This is to be Christologically and anthropologically affirmed. Our present experiences compel us to eschatological affirmations. The problem with this method is to what extent human experiences can be definitive in the search for meaning and mystery of life. This is mainly because of the divergent ways in which human beings experience the same reality in life. Sometimes it depends on our convictions in life, the values we hold, and also our conceptual framework.

c. Eschatological Anticipation

Anticipation or 'prolepsis' is a recent eschatological category. Prolepsis has its roots in Greek epistemology. In Greek mythology, it denotes pre-concepts and anticipatory images. These are considered as 'search images' for new experiences. Husserl is the main advocate of this method. According to him, anticipation has the essential structure of cognition. The opposite of prolepsis is anachronism. To be proleptic means to be ahead of one's times. The Biblical foundation here is the Easter experience of the early church. In order to be ahead of our times, we have to be historically rooted and Biblically grounded.

3. Schools of thought in Eschatology

Efforts have been made to identify a few schools of thought in eschatological thinking. The discussions are mostly centered around the theological significance of history, the role of socio-political movements for transformation in history, the relationship between the divine and human in the historical process, and so on. What follows is only a brief description of each school and its emphasis.

a. Consistent Eschatology

Schweitzer and M. Werner are the main advocates of this school. According to them, Jesus' teaching was apocalyptic, and it was nullified by the ongoing character of history. Therefore, the meaning of history should be sought elsewhere. This is not a holistic understanding of the life and ministry of Christ. Even though there are apocalyptic references in the ministry of Jesus Christ, he was always for a prophetic eschatology. Rather than making predictions, he addressed the dire needs and struggles of human life. In other words, he always reflected 'the human face of God.'

b. Realised Eschatology

C. H. Dodd, the main proponent of this school pointed out that the final consummation has occurred in the coming of Christ. The reign of God has fully arrived in Christ and since Christ there is only a slow expansion of the reign of God in the world. It has been pointed out that in the later writings of Dodd, he posits that there are futuristic elements of Christian faith and there is significance in the mission work of the church for the manifestation of the church. According to Leonardo Boff, Jesus is realized eschatology, and as such he represents the end of history in a two fold sense: First, history has reached it's end in the sense of end, in the sense of goal. There is nothing more to be hoped for, savifically, that has not happened, in Jesus who lived, died and raised again. Second: History has reached it's end in the sense of fullness, since Jesus' resurrection is the fulfillment of the human being in God.[7] Here it should be noted that the present and the futuristic dimensions are to be seen as two sides of the same coin in Christian eschatology.

c. Salvation History (*Heilgeschichte*)

This is an interpretation based on the Biblical understanding of the consummation of the world. Here God is present and active to reveal His will, which begins with creation and in the return of Christ to be followed by judgment and consummation. Irenaeus, Augustine, and a few reformers were of this view. The main proponent of this view in the last century was Oscar Cullmann. According to him history is linear in nature, and hence the whole of world history is included in the salvation history. He considers the church as the bearer of this salvation history. The question is whether Cullmann is claiming too much for the church. Is the church the 'bearer of salvation or one of God's instruments of salvation'?

d. Dialectical School

This is a continuation of the dialectical theology of Barth and Brunner. Here, the relation between time and history, between God and the world are seen in dialectical terms. Rather than the end of history, the focus here is the eternal meaning of each moment in history. The attempt here is to find both God's *yes* and *no* to every moment of history. The question here is how to discern God's *yes* and *no* in history. Is it not possible that some times, God's *yes* can be construed as *no* and vice-versa?

e. Existentialist School

The main figure here is Bultmann and his system is with in his theological frame work known as "Demythologization." His approach is similar to that of the realised eschatology of Dodd. In his system, more emphasis is given to the decision of the individual's every moment and his existential experience. Church is considered as an eschatological community here. It's true that Paul Tillich makes a distinction between authentic existence and inauthentic existence; and he finds the authentic existence in Christ. Over against the Western philosophical notion of Descartes, "I think, therefore I exist"; in existentialism, it's "I exist, therefore I think." Here the emphasis is on human subjectivity and also the concept that existence precedes essence. Existential theologians like Paul Tillich was of the view that in order to speak of God, one must first examine human existence. Here the category of human existence is considered as the best way to reflect on Christian doctrines. While acknowledging the basic fact that the human existence could be a useful vehicle for conveying the Christian message, it should be noted that the atheistic element of existentialism is not conducive to Christian theology.

f. School of Hope

The main figure here is Jurgen Moltmann. Moltmann is known for his remarkable contributions in the field of eschatology. The focus of his system is the crucifixion and resurrection of Jesus Christ. The human response to this Christ event is Christian hope, which has the following elements: the mission of the church to all nations, the hunger for righteousness, the struggle for public obedience to God, and love for the true life of the imperilled and impaired creation.[8] The question here is whether Christian hope is merely human response to the Christ event. What is the place of God's grace here ? Even though human response to God is essential in Christian faith, it should be noted that hope is God's doing within us, and human task is to discern God's work in the world and to be agents of hope at all levels. This theme will be discussed in the upcoming sections of this book, especially Chapter 14, "Church as a community of hope."

g. School of Liberation

There are several thinkers in this area, both Liberation theologians of Latin America as well as Indian theologians. Among the Indian theologians, M. M. Thomas' contributions need special mention here. Thomas is known for his theological reflections on the socio-political significance of Christ and also for his attempts to discern the presence of Christ in contemporary Liberation movements for justice, freedom, and human rights. But he never absolutized any of the movements. His words of caution in this field are as follows: *Jesus Christ is also at work in the revolutions as victory over the evil forces through his cross and resurrection. His Kingdom and the New Humanity are offered within the revolution as the fulfilment of its promise. Therefore, the promise of Christ or a richer human life for men (sic.) will be fulfilled only if the revolution receives within it Christ's Gospel of Redemption and New Creation of which the church is a witness.*[9]

In other words, he rightly recognizes that revolutions can have within them self-righteousness and idolatrous elements which are likely to betray their promise of a new social order. Hence, a credible Christian response to such movements involves a critical and selective participation and also a prophetic criticism of their idolatrous elements in the name of Christ.

4. Historical Development of Eschatology

It is to be admitted that there is a historical development of eschatology. Right from the New Testament times, there have been attempts in this regard by many in different ecclesial traditions. The churches have accepted and incorporated some and rejected others. Even though this historical development of eschatology is not the main thrust of this work, some historical references are inevitable, mainly to show the shift in the articulation of this topic and its continuum as a doctrine of the church.

Immediately after the New Testament times, the patristic era was preoccupied with the *parousia*, the second coming of Christ, resurrection, judgment, and so on. Another concern of this period was the status of the dead, the role of the dead in the economy of salvation, etc. During this period, death was considered not only simply as the wages of sin as Paul says, but as the remedy of sin.

The middle ages witnessed the following developments: dualism between the body and soul, and the doctrine of the immortality of the soul. On the whole, the emphasis during this period is the individualistic eschatology at the expense of the social dimension of it. One such development is the doctrine of purgatory, mainly in the 12th century, as a state between heaven and hell, which has its place in the Roman Catholic tradition even to this day. The Eastern tradition doesn't approve this even though it has the concept of the church as a 'community of the living and the dead.' One of the aberrations of this concept led to the notorious 'sale of indulgences', which was vehemently challenged by Martin Luther in the 16th century, in the context of Reformation. During the post-reformation period, due to the influence of Enlightenment in the eighteenth and early nineteenth centuries, "...eschatology was almost reduced to naturalistic Theology." The possibility of God's intervention in the affairs of this world, the concern for consummation were challenged by many Enlightenment thinkers. On the whole, one of the contributions of Vatican II is the attempt to overcome the separation between the individual and social dimensions in eschatology.

The main developments in the field of Eschatology are in the 20th century. It is to be specially noted that eschatology in the 20th century was in the context of the horrors of the two World Wars and also the Jewish holocaust under the Nazi regime in Germany. The contributions of Vatican II, especially two of its documents, the *Pastoral Constitution of the Church in the Modern World* and the *Dogmatic Constitution on the Church* and the some of the documents of WCC Assemblies are commendable here. Both documents of Vatican II focus on the renewal of the creation by the work of the Holy Spirit, and also underscore the human efforts to build a better world and the struggle for justice within the eschatological plan of God. Several of the WCC Assembly themes also reiterate this theme such as "Come Holy Spirit and Renew the Creation", Canberra Assembly theme, 1991; "Turn to God and Rejoice in Hope", Harrare Assembly, 1998.

Besides the General Assemblies of WCC, the contributions of the Commission on "Church and Society" are also remarkable. One such consultation was on "The Creative role of Science and Faith." The consultation was at the Massachusetts Institute of Technology in July1979. The theme of the consultation was "Faith and Science in an Unjust World." Over 400 participants, scientists, theologians and Biblical scholars from 56 countries took part in the deliberations.

At this consultation, Dr. Ruben Alves from Brazil presented a paper "On the Eating Habits of Science"! In a parabolic style he portrayed the scientists and technologists as wolves and ordinary people as lambs. Alves had two crucial points:

One: Science has developed a series of accounts of what it is. These accounts, most of the time, hide its eating habits.

Two: Lambs know more about the wolves than wolves do. A wolf is, to a lamb, what the wolf does to the lamb, and not what the wolf thinks he is doing.[10]

On the whole, the consultation came down heavily on the absolutist claims of modern science and technology especially its methodology of rational objectivity and value-free pursuit of truth.

Another important issue was the transfer of science and technology, which is an international market of exploitation. Now it is generally understood that some of the socio-ethical issues raised by modern science and technology cannot be solved by scientists and technologists alone. The consultation was for an issue-based dialogue between science and faith. The traditional claim of science as pure objective knowledge without an element of subjectivity has been questioned by several scientists and theologians. The question that comes to the fore here is whether in the process of knowing does the knower stand on his own or does he participate in the object of knowledge. The problem with modern scientific and technological culture is that all realities of life are reduced to quantifiable and marketable commodities. It seems as if that which is not saleable or marketable is of no value! Hence, what human beings are tempted to think is that they are not limited.

These are definitely attempts within the field of the wider concerns in Eschatology in the 20th Century; the concern for the pro-life sentiments in the field of science and technology and also the concern for a just and egalitarian world. Contributions from two Western authors that stand out in the field of eschatology in the 20th century, or perhaps contemporary eschatology are Jurgen Moltmann's work (especially *Theology of Hope* and *The Coming of God*) and Bishop N. T. Wright's work (especially *Surprised by Hope* and *History and Eschatology*). Both of their attempts are broadly in the field of Prophetic eschatology. They have brought eschatology to the centre of theological endeavour.

3

Eschatology and Biblical Hermeneutics

This chapter is a thorough discussion on the relationship between eschatology and Biblical hermeneutics. The author acknowledges both the use and abuse of the Bible in the history of the church. The first part is a review of some of the existing interpretations, especially in the end time and New generation groups. The second part has to do with the main sources of interpretation; the way the sources have functioned in the different church traditions and a contemporary reading of the sources. The last part is an analysis of the basics of Biblical interpretation. Here a clear distinction is made between the Word of God and the words of the Bible, and also the fundamentals of the Bible and Biblical fundamentalism.

The area of Biblical hermeneutics is so vast and any attempt to go onto the details is beyond the scope of this book. Nevertheless, the attempt here is to highlight a few areas of Biblical interpretation, which have a direct bearing on the topic of this work. Here it is to be recognized that the Bible has been used and abused in the historical tradition of the Church. The Bible has been used in a variety of ways; such as a devotional book, a study book, a book for personal consolation in times of crisis situations of life, as a piece of literature, as a weapon for moral and political claims and so on. The basic question here are the following: How should we approach the Bible? How should we interpret the Bible? What is the place of the Bible in Christian tradition? Does the Bible have a decisive role in our journey of faith? Is the Bible to be seen as a blue-print for action or a pattern of obedience to God? Here it is to be acknowledged that there is no consensus on these issues among the churches. The attempt here is only to go into some of the crucial areas; especially on the question of the relationship between Eschatology and Hermeneutics.

1. A Few Issues in Biblical Interpretation

There are Biblical literalists who would claim, "I have no theology. What I am offering is the pure Word of God." Just a few Biblical references would reveal the fallacy of this approach. In 1Corinthians 3, Paul says,

> *But, brothers, I could not address you as spiritual people, but as people of the flesh, as infants in Christ. I fed you with milk, not solid food, for you were not ready for it; and even now you are not yet ready* (vs.1-3).

Here the contrast is between those who are mature in the knowledge of Christ and those who are 'spiritually deficient or illiterate.' The same contrast is found in the letter to Hebrews.

> *For though by this time you ought to be teachers, you need someone to teach you again, the basic principles of the oracles of God. You need milk, not solid food; for everyone who lives on milk is unskilled in the word of righteousness, since he is a child. For solid food is for the mature, for those who have their powers of discernment trained by constant practice to distinguish good from evil* (Heb.5:12-14).

In other words, the writer is not happy with the spiritual superficiality of the believers. Though the name of the letter to Hebrews is not given in the book, it is believed that the immediate readers of the book were the converts from Judaism.

The problem within several of our churches is that our people are educated and enlightened in all fields, except Bible and Theology. I am reminded of one of my church members, a Professor of Biology, who once said, "When I am in College Campus, I am with Darwin. I have no problem teaching the Theory of Evolution. But when I am in church campus, I cling on to the Biblical truth." This kind of a dual existence is very common among the New Generation and end time groups. Unfortunately, several of the clergy leave their theological studies and convictions, when they leave the Seminary! Only a few would pursue their studies and build on the foundations they have received from their formal theological education. Even among the theologically trained also, the above kind of dual existence is very common.

Academic excellence or expertise at the expense of a life of commitment in the community is counter productive. In our educational field there is no dearth of experts. The question to be asked is whether one is really committed, concerned, and compassionate in life. The problem with many of our youth is that they fail to integrate their knowledge in the field of natural and human sciences with their faith and Biblical insights. Hence, when it comes to an in depth study of the Word of God or issues of faith or reflections on contemporary socio-ethical issues, either they opt for a simplistic faith or negate faith.

Frequently, some of the references in Paul's letters, especially in Corinthians are also misunderstood more often than properly understood. For example, in 1 Corinthians1, he says:

> *For the word of the cross is folly to those who are perishing, but to us who are being saved it is the power of God. For it is written; I will destroy the wisdom of the wise, and the discernment of the discerning, I will thwart. Where is the one who is wise? Where is the scribe? Where is the debater of this age? Has not God made foolish the wisdom of this world? For since, in the wisdom of God, the world did not know God through wisdom, it pleased God through the folly of what we preach, to save those who believe. For Jews demand signs and Greeks seek wisdom, but we preach Christ crucified a stumbling block to the Jews, and folly to Gentiles* (1Cor.1:18-23).

The usual interpretation given to this text by the Biblical literalists and end time prophets go as follows: "There is no need to interpret the Word of God; we have to take it literally. Interpretation is the wisdom of this world; what we need is heavenly wisdom." But Biblical scholars point out that what Paul is negating here is the Greek notion of wisdom, which was prevalent in the form of Gnosticism in the early church. This school of thought was influenced by Greek philosophy and its 'Logos tradition.' The word *logos* was used by the Greek philosopher, Heraclitus (535-475 BC) for the impersonal cosmic principle. Philo of Alexandria, a contemporary of St. Paul translated it as "The Word of God." St. John took over this concept and gave the meaning "The Word (Logos) became flesh and dwelt among us" (Jn.1:14). In other words, St. John gives a new dimension to the Greek wisdom. Here it is to be acknowledged that there is a strong Wisdom tradition in Judaism and some of the Old Testament books such as Proverbs and Job are from that tradition. In other words, in Judaism and Christian faith, Wisdom is given by God. This is the reason why the patristic Fathers said: "Christian faith is intellectual illumination." In 1Corinthians 14, Paul recognizes this positive role of wisdom: "*For what am I to do then? I will pray with my spirit and I will pray with my mind also. I will sing praise with my spirit, but I will sing with my mind also*"(Vs.15).

This is part of Paul's exhortation to the spiritual enthusiasts in Corinth. In other words, with our knowledge and wisdom, we can do two things: Think that you and I are self-sufficient and you can comprehend everything with your reason. This was the norm during the period of Enlightenment in the West. This is considered as the so-called "autonomy of human reason." The second approach is the basic awareness that your reason is given by God for the edification of the community. But, the problem is that the Biblical literalists won't allow you to think and reason out. The reasons are obvious: Their so-called authority and claims will be challenged!

Now, let me briefly bring out some of the Biblical interpretations that we need to challenge.

a. Allegoric Interpretation

St. Augustine (354-430 A.D) is considered to be the chief proponent of this method. He is known for his writing "The City of God and the city of Man", written against the backdrop of the fall of the Roma Empire. According to him, there is a clear distinction between the eternal city of God and the temporal city of man; hence these two are rival entities. Martin Luther took over this concept from Augustine and developed his "Two Kingdom theory", namely: "The Kingdom of God and the Kingdom of man." He makes a distinction between the civic Kingdom and the spiritual Kingdom. Though Augustine and Luther made significant contributions in their respective areas and contexts; the concept of the "City of God /man" and "Kingdom of God/man" is dualistic in nature and hence it doesn't do justice to the Biblical truth in its totality. It is beyond the scope of this section to go into the details of these concepts here.

There are scholars who are of the view that Augustine was influenced by the Gnostic tradition where the allegoric form of Biblical interpretation was common. They also believed that there were deeper and hidden truths in the Bible that were not accessible to the ordinary believers.

This is how he interprets the Parable of the good Samaritan: The journey from Jerusalem to Jericho means one's journey from the holy place to an unholy place; the wounded person on the roadside is a sinner; the good Samaritan represents Christ; the inn is the church and the wine and oil represent baptism; the two coins given to the inn keeper represent the Old and New Testaments of the Bible and so on! Ever since Augustine, this method of interpretation has been the one followed by the literal Biblicists in history. The problem with this approach is that there is always an attempt to see the hidden meanings behind the Biblical texts. Similarly, this approach doesn't recognize the context of Biblical narratives.

The context of this Biblical narrative needs special attention. A question was posed to Jesus by a Jewish lawyer: "Who is my neighbor?" (Lk. 10:29) Here it is to be noted that for a Jew, a neighbor is only a Jew. He would never consider a Samaritan as his neighbor or friend. There are several historical reasons for this communal divide between the Jews and the Samaritans. According to Biblical scholars, the chief one is that the Samaritans didn't recognize Jerusalem as the abode of Yahweh; their place of worship was Gerizim. This is evident in the conversation of Jesus with the Samaritan woman (Jn. 4:20) Through this parable, Jesus is addressing the issue of Jewish exclusivism and perfectionism. In the end, he praises the action of the Samaritan, and the Jewish lawyer is exhorted to emulate the action of the Samaritan. Since that time, in the history of the Church, he is called the "Good Samaritan"! Hence, the need is to contextualize this parable; to see if similar 'ethnic slurs' or caste discriminations are found in the church or in the community. Such an approach would open up a new horizons in the hermeneutical task in our times. For example, the issue of Apartheid in South Africa, Black Liberation movement in U.S, Dalit movement in India and so on. In other words, the challenge here is a systemic understanding of the Bible and search for its relevance.

b. Otherworldly Interpretation

Here, a dichotomy is made between this world and the other world and life in the other world is interpreted as the real one; and life on earth is some kind of 'an inevitable state'; a place of preparation for eternal life. This approach is found in most of our church traditions; especially this theology looms large in the conventions. The problem with this approach is that here the world that God created and loved is negated. Similarly, our discipleship on earth is also ignored. This is also a negation of the Biblical God who is in the world; the incarnate Jesus who took his earthly life and its challenges seriously, and also our task as God's co-workers in the world.

c. Individualistic Interpretation

Biblical texts are quoted out of context here; context in which the texts are written and context now. The issue here is that Bible is almost portrayed as a magical book; and its reading is considered as an end in itself. Personality cult is very strong in almost all New Generation churches. Most of the groups are centered on the charisma of an individual. Very often, such an individual creates a trust with his own family members, for the purpose of registration. Absolute secrecy is one of the main characteristics of this tradition. Individualistic visions, truth claims, and revelations are the hallmarks of this group.

d. Polemical Interpretation

All these groups project Satan or some other forces as an agent working against the believers. All those who criticize the leadership, their financial sources, or accounts are always cursed and condemned to hell. The strategy is always to create an attitude of fear among the devotees so that they will always be subservient to the leadership gimmicks. The ethical question here is whether the Bible can be used as a tool for polemics. Rather, what we need is continuous struggle against all forces of sin and evil that are embedded in our systems and institutions.

e. Dogmatic Interpretation

In the history of the Church, dogmas have had a significance, especially in the context of some of the heresies. Those dogmas were in a way, defensive in nature. Here a distinction has to be made between a 'dogma' and 'dogmatism.' If dogma is part of the life and witness of the church as the affirmations of the basic tenets of faith; dogmatism is the attitude of self-sufficiency of a particular dogma and the unwillingness to revise it in the light of contextual challenges and needs. All the Biblical literalists thrive on some dogmas; mostly adult baptism, individualistic revelations, anointing of the Holy Spirit, speaking in tongues, end time predictions, etc. Surprisingly, some of these groups won't allow the adherents to change their church membership; for them it is only for the satisfaction of the social needs.

2. Main Sources of Interpretation

Only three main sources are discussed here: Authority, Tradition, and Inspiration.

a. The Question of Authority

Ever since the beginning of Christian Church, attempts have been made to interpret the Biblical authority. The main line churches have always maintained the view that the Bible is the Word of God in the words of human beings. In other words, on the one hand the Bible is a divine document; and on the other hand, it's a human document. Paul's exhortation to Timothy is "*All Scripture is breathed out by God, and profitable for teaching, for reproof, for correction, and for training in righteousness that the man of God may be complete.*" (2 Tim. 3:16-17). In the Mar Thoma liturgy for Holy Communion, this text is sung by the Choir immediately after the reading of the Gospel. In a way, Paul says that the authority of the Word is in four areas: For teaching, for reproof, for correction and for training in righteousness. In other words, the Biblical writers didn't have before them several of our socio-political or ethical issues. So, when we say the Bible has answers to all questions; what do we mean? Here we have to make a distinction between the words of the Bible and the Word of God. J. R. Chandran, the former Principal of the United Theological College, Bangalore, always used to tell his students that "the Bible contains the Word of God." In an article, "The Authority of the Bible for Christian Social Action", after negating some of the traditional approaches such as, Biblical literalism, proof-text and so on, he points out that "*It is an existential, moral and spiritual authority and not an abstract legal authority.*"[1] The question is whether a *sola scriptura* approach is possible in any church tradition. This is not to underestimate the authority of the Word of God. Duraisingh, reflects on the authority of the Scripture as follows:

> *The claim of the absolute and sole authority in doctrinal matters in protestant churches is a dubious and dangerous one. It is dubious because, if one is honest, one has to accept that the ultimate authority for Protestants is not and never has been scripture alone; but scripture as interpreted in the tradition of their respective denomination or school of thought.*[2]

This questions the popular notion that *sola scriptura* is the norm that looms large in all Protestant traditions. It is also a protest against an attempt to make

Christian faith into the 'religion of a book.What is of great importance here is to see the authority of the Bible as its intrinsic and relational value. In other words, the question is how does the Bible become decisive and significant in the life of the community of faith? What matters here is the illuminating and relational dimension of the Word in our real-life situations in the journey of faith.

There have been attempts to highlight some of the corrective measures and self-critical elements within the Bible in the discussion on the authority of the Bible. The Faith and Order consultation of WCC at Louvain in 1971, took note of this process of reinterpretation within the Bible. The document of the consultation points out:

> *Just as the Biblical writers responded to a particular situation, so contemporary interpretation must also be determined by our situation. The questions which are put to the text play a large part in the interpretation. Of course, the text has its own weight. It poses its own questions and some questions which spring from our own situation will find no echo in the Bible.*[3]

What is of great importance here is the perspective with which we interpret the Biblical narratives. Here we are invited to stand under the horizon of the Word. What we need is a basic awareness that the Bible is not to be seen as a 'treasury of gifts' given to us for our use when we need, rather as Hans Ruedi Weber rightly points out: "It's the book that reads me"! Along with that, let me say it's the book that challenges us, motivates us, admonishes us, and commissions us.

b. The Question of Tradition

The emphasis on "Scripture within the Tradition of the Church" is found mostly among the Roman Catholic and Eastern schools of thought. Here tradition basically means, the tradition of faith, the tradition of witness to the scripture in the community. In the Biblical tradition we have two communities: the community of Israel and the community of the early church. Jarslov Pelikan, the Eastern thinker makes a distinction between "tradition and traditionalism. According to him, "Tradition is the living faith of the dead; traditionalism is the dead faith of the living." In a way, the Biblical narratives are the people's responses to God in their journey of life, their obedience to God as well as disobedience, their struggles, aspirations, and hope.

Hans George Gadamer, in his book *Truth and Method*, makes some valuable observations on tradition. Regarding the important role of tradition, its subjective assimilation and to the inevitable pre-understanding (prejudice), he observes:

> *We stand always within tradition, and this is no objectifying process, i.e., we do not conceive of what tradition says as something other, something alien. It is always part of us, a model or exemplar, a recognition of*

ourselves which our later historical judgment would hardly see as a kind of knowledge, but as the simplest preservation of tradition.[4]

While recognizing the value of tradition in Biblical hermeneutics, a question can be raised as to whether our concern should be the 'preservation of tradition', or its re-examination and an attempt to recapture its cardinal virtues.

In line with the Eastern Orthodox position, Mar Gregorios sheds light on the inevitability of tradition in our hermeneutical efforts in India in the following words: *Any fruitful Indian discussion on hermeneutics must take into account the fact that scripture cannot be interpreted apart from tradition.*[5]

A realistic understanding of tradition is not always backward looking or clinging on to the rigid systems of the past. The concern should be to bring out the essential meaning of the text in the light of new situational challenges. In other words, the concern should be to bring to the fore "the continuing life of the community as a valid category in order to reach new meaning." Tradition (*sampradaya*), here becomes the bearer and endower (*tatparya*) of meaning.[6]

Nevertheless, tradition understood in its dogmatic, authoritarian, institutional, or hierarchical nature is of little relevance in our contemporary hermeneutical efforts.

While acknowledging the position of the 'scripture within the tradition of the church' over and against the '*sola scriptura*' attitude that is dominant in the protestant tradition vis-à-vis the New Generation churches and end time groups, some critical remarks are inevitable. What is the possible check on this tradition? What is the guarantee that an over emphasis on the role of tradition will not lead to traditionalism, dogmatism, and rigidity in the life of the church? After all, whose tradition are we talking about: The tradition of the people who are in actual life situations and struggles or the tradition of Episcopal hierarchy? If more emphasis is given to the tradition of the 'wider community of faith', then some of the living, protest traditions, also should be given due attention. Creative tradition should always be oriented towards the future. The concern should not be to give infallibility or sacrosanctity to any of the ancient or modern traditions, but a genuine attempt to recapture the significant values of tradition that are useful in our innovative steps in the hermeneutical endeavour.

c. The Question of Inspiration

The concept of scriptural inspiration has been understood in a variety of ways in the different ecclesial traditions. At the very outset, let me point out that the Holy Spirit is the real interpreter of the Word. The Holy Spirit has been active in the world prior to the formation of the scripture, during the process of formation of it, and after the formation of the Bible.

There has been a proliferation of theories, claims, and counter claims on the question of the inspiration of the scriptures. There are some New Generation churches which always claim supremacy of their interpretations in the light of the way in which they understand the inspiration of the Bible. The concept of inspiration and the Christian affirmation of the Bible as the 'Word of God' are interrelated. In the context of the inspiration of the Bible, the 'Word of God' should be understood in the tradition of the prophetic word, (Jer. 1:9,12; Isa. 55:10-11)and of the meaning of the Word in the New Testament writings (2 Thess. 3:1; Heb. 4:12-13). "That is, as a dialogue between God and man(sic.), and at the same time a divine power, within man (sic.) and history, to make the message it contains to become a reality."[7] When we proclaim the Bible as the word of God in the words of human beings, the divine and human elements in the Bible are duly acknowledged. The task before us, then is to make it alive and inspirational in our times. Karl Barth gives four meanings to the Word of God: The spoken word in creation, the incarnate word in Jesus Christ, the revealed Word in history, and the written Word.

The infallibility of the word of God is to be seen within the framework of the concept of Inspiration. As pointed out earlier, this is to be seen with the basic affirmation that the Bible is a divine as well as a human document. This means that the message (divine document) is mediated through human language, symbols, metaphors, and imageries; and these are subjected to error and corrections. This is the reason why we have different translations and editions of the Bible. Some of the end time proponents have created their own edition of the Bible and they make exclusive claims about it.

As mentioned earlier, what is to be underscored here is the search for the inspiration of the scripture within the salvific plan of God. As Clovodis Boff suggests:

> We need not look for formulas to copy, or techniques to apply from the scripture. What the scripture will offer us are rather something like orientations, models, types, directives, principles, inspiration… What we need is the capacity to judge, on our own initiative, in our own right-according to the mind of Christ, or according to the Spirit, the new, unpredictable situations, with which we are continuously confronted.[8]

In other words, what the scripture gives us is a pattern of obedience to God as concrete historical human beings. Our attempt to highlight the question of inspiration should not lead us to literal Biblicism or 'Bibliolatry' or Biblical fundamentalism. Rather, the concern should always be to go beyond the words of the Bible to the underlying spirit.

3. The Basics of Biblical Interpretation

The main argument of the Biblical literalists' is that the Bible says so and you just take it. They won't even care whether the text was written in a particular context; and perhaps, the primary readers had some faith issues etc. Here it should be noted that the Bible was written by people who were inspired by the Spirit of God. The Biblical narratives are mainly retrospective documents. The Spirit of God has been active before the formation of the Bible; both in its oral and written traditions and after the completion of the Bible. Hence, the Holy Spirit is the real interpreter of the Word of God.

Two negative approaches are to be noted here: proof text approach and Bibliolatry. There are Christians who believe that the Bible gives answers to all questions that human beings ask. Well, here we have to remind ourselves that the Biblical writers didn't have before them many of our contemporary issues and as Dr. Stanley Samartha rightly reminds us: *"The Bible gives us a pattern of obedience and not a blue-print for action."*

Bibliolatry is even more problematic. It is some sort of a worshipping attitude towards the Bible without going into the depth of it. The question here is wheher we are prepared to go deeper than the letters of the Bible.

a. Two Approaches

Sola scriptura (Bible alone) and Bible within the tradition of faith. As pointed out earlier, the first approach is found mostly among the congregational churches and the second mostly in the Eastern tradition of faith. In the first, the interpretation is mainly literal, otherworldly, and individualistic. In the Eastern ecclesial tradition, the Bible is understood as the faith affirmations of the early Christian communities. Here the event has primacy over the text.

Hence, '*sola scriptura*' is not possible. The basic question to be asked here is whether the Bible is *a source of faith* or *a witness of faith.* In the *sola scriptura* approach, the Bible is the source of faith whereas in the Eastern tradition, it's a witness of faith.

b. Biblical Worldview

Biblical worldview involves three elements:

1. Belief system: e.g. Three-layer concept of the world, Israel as the only chosen people of God, diseases are due to demon possession, women do not have the same social status as men etc. All of us are born within a particular cultural milieu. Our world-view gives us certain myths and meaning systems. A Biblical example is Mtt. 14:22-35 where the disciples fail to understand their master. When Jesus approaches them in the midst of a crisis, the immediate response surprisingly is "It is a demon and screamed with fear"! This shows that the disciples were enslaved by a cultural myth, which says that the ocean is the citadel of evil and satanic powers, which is not within the purview of God's salvific regime. Biblical scholars would say that the purpose of this "nature miracle of Jesus" was to challenge this myth and to prove his sovereignty over the whole creation.

4. Symbol System

All symbols are products of culture. There are verbal as well as non-verbal symbols and in all cultures special meanings are attributed to certain symbols: e.g. Right hand side is considered to be good and left hand side is considered to be bad. Even we say that God's right hand side symbolizes life and salvation and left symbolizes condemnation and judgment (Mtt. 25:31-46). Based on this literal understanding of the Bible, in Kerala aborted attempts are made by parents to change the left handlers to the right! The girls are mostly the sufferers here and the justification is that they are to serve on tables. (As if boys can't serve on tables at home!). There should be a continuous rediscovery of the meaning of Biblical symbols in each situation. For example, how would the blacks look at the traditional view of the 'white as the symbol of purity and the black as the symbol of evil is a question to be noted? There should be a continuous rediscovery of the meaning of Biblical symbols in each situation.

5. Value System

All values are caught; they are never taught. Values are basically two-fold: instrumental and intrinsic. Our lives have both these values: e.g., our family status, job, and education, social positions-all belong to the instrumental; whereas our character, lifestyle, commitment, and faith life etc., comprise of the intrinsic. When we make choices in life, especially when we look for a life-partner, which are the dominant criteria? Ancient Jewish society had several social taboos which were discriminatory in nature; for example, those who do some jobs are sinners, the shepherds, tax collectors etc. It was believed that diseases were due to demon possession; skin diseases like leprosy were considered as stigmatized ones. In the New Testament we read how Jesus transcends those taboos through his miracles/ signs of the Kingdom.

a. Eternal and Temporal Values

What we need is the spirit of discernment to distinguish between what is temporal and what is eternal. For example, in Rom.13:1ff, Paul advises the church to be "*subject to the authorities for all authorities come from God.*" Here authority means the state of Rome. Does Paul intend to give us here an eternal doctrine about the Christian approach to the State? If the state becomes demonic and oppressive what should we do? A brief survey of the historical context will show that the persecution of the church by the Roman Empire was not severe in those days and Paul was mostly persecuted by his own people. Paul even enjoyed the privilege of Roman citizenship in those days.Where as in Rev. 13 the same state of Rome is portrayed as a monster and the faithful are summoned to struggle against such an evil force. Similarly, when he says, "Women should be silent in the church..." is he addressing an immediate concern among the spiritual enthusiasts in Corinth or is he supporting patriarchy and its norms?

b. People of Faith

We have to distinguish between 'the fundamentals of the Bible' and 'Biblical fundamentalism.' There are sociologists who are of the view that the origin of fundamentalism is mainly in the West, in the form of Christian fundamentalism. The special edition on "*Religious Fundamentalism: An Asian Perspective*", sheds light on the origin and growth of fundamentalism in different religious traditions. In an article on "*A Christian Understanding of Fundamentalism*", the author says:

> "*Fundamentalism can be attributed to a group or individuals, who when reading the Bible, are more concerned with finding their own Gospel, than in discovering its (as yet) unknown message. Christian identity depends here on an acquired grasp of the divine identity sometimes integrated to a level of fantasy (as in the more or less conscious identification of one or another of its preachers with Christ)-an image which tends to realize itself in positivism.*"[9]

As mentioned earlier, Biblical fundamentalism has always had tragic ethical consequences in the community. Like any other notion of fundamentalism, in Biblical fundamentalism also the basic concerns are the protection of the *statusquo*, exclusive truth claims, personality cults, and intolerance to the Main Line Church traditions and people of other faiths and ideologies.

The Bible contains God's agenda for this world. It is not to be seen as the private property of the church; it is a record of God's concern for this world and human response to it in history. Any attempt to interpret the Bible without the mindset of Christ should be challenged. Let us allow ourselves to be enriched, motivated, and challenged by the Word of God. God is not bound by what he has done in the past. He has His own ways of doing things in this world. An interpretation of the written Word must always be associated with an experiential appropriation through visualizing the Biblical events, personalizing, and contextualizing those events in our concrete situations of life. The question for us to ponder on is whether we have the preparedness to listen to the promptings of the Holy Spirit who opens new possibilities before us in our journey of faith.

4

What does the "End" mean?

The word "'End" is misunderstood in most of the church traditions than properly understood. The Greek word for "End," *Telos* means culmination, fulfillment, consummation etc. In other words, the end is not annihilation or a cosmic catastrophe; it's transformation of the created order. This is the basic vision that Jesus had in his life and mission. Two occasions when the question regarding the "end" was posed to Jesus in Matthew 24 and Acts.1and Jesus' responses are analyzed in this chapter. The task of the church here is a proper edification at different levels. We need both Biblical insights and theological perspectives in this task. It is to be noted that very little is done in this area in the main line church traditions; and hence people are using mostly the end time teachers' materials which are freely available.

In Christian spiritual circles very often two approaches are found in this regard. One approach says let us wait and see the future. Another approach says the future should be brought into the present. Here it should be remembered that the answers to these ultimate questions can be expressed only in symbolic and poetic language. Two elements are to be noted here are imagination and vision. Nevertheless, individualistic imaginations and visions, which are alienated from the community of faith should not be entertained.

Moltmann finds the following meanings to the concept:

One: The Nuclear End time. This is characterized by the methods of mass destruction. It is as if we are living at a time when the end of humanity can be brought about at any minute. The examples of Hiroshima and Nagasaki should not be ignored. On August 6th, 1945, America dropped the first atom bomb on Hiroshima. Three days later, on August 9th, Nagasaki was atom bombed. The two bombs killed over three lakhs fifty thousand people and made over two lakhs fifty thousand traumatized and there are such survivors even today! Mahatma Gandhi called it an empty victory and a crime against humanity. Now scientists say that the nuclear bombs with the nuclear powers of the world can destroy the world several times! Even now the nuclear powers are competing each other to establish their authority.

Two: The Ecological End time. This is characterized by the destruction of the earth mainly due to the belief that nature is for human consumption. We stand in need of a paradigm shift here from an anthropocentric to a life-centred approach. In other words, a basic awareness that the created order is not for us to plunder and loot but rather that we are part of it. Those who live in Kerala are keenly aware of the pollution of several of the rivers, especially the Pampa river which has been the platform for three important spiritual events: Sabarimala pilgrimage, Cherukolpuzha Hindu religious convention, and the Maramon Convention of the Mar Thoma Church. Notwithstanding some of the efforts at the last Maramon Convention to make it plastic free, the Mar Thoma Church never took it as a matter of Confession!

Three: The Economic End time. This is characterized by the impoverishment of the third world. This is mainly through trade policies, globalization, and its market ideology. Slave trade, cheap labour, violation of basic human rights, and wars were rampant during the last century.

> *"Like a huge idol, like the beast in Revelation13, the present economic system covers the earth with its open sewer of unemployment and homelessness, hunger and nakedness, despair and death...The Beast has become a ravening monster, armed to the teeth with arms and guns, atomic bombs, warships with computer guided radar systems and satellites, and it is bringing humanity to the verge of total and sudden annihilation."*[1] Gen. Omar Bradley points out in a subtle way this predicament of the modern scientific world.
>
> "*We have too many men of science, too few men of God. We have grasped the mystery of the atom and rejected the Sermon on the Mount. The world has achieved brilliance without wisdom, power without conscience. Ours is a world of nuclear giants and ethical infants. We know more about war than we know about peace, more about killing than about living.*"

Nevertheless, the problem with many of our intellectuals is that they fail to integrate their scientific knowledge with faith. Some would even see faith within the realm of 'heart' and science and technology within the realm of 'reason.' Hence, either they negate faith or opt for a blind faith. As mentioned earlier, this dichotomy between the spiritual and the secular could be due to the influence of the Greek dualistic thinking. Contemporary theological enterprise would not allow such a dichotomy; rather it seeks out points of convergence between the two. As Tertullian, the Greek philosopher-convert rightly reminds us: "An unconsecrated reason is devilish."

Christian faith is not faith in God as an object; He is our eternal subject. In the Eastern theological tradition, faith is intellectual illumination, which would enable us to discern the pro-life, and the anti-life sentiments in all areas of life on earth. In the wider sense of the term, as the late Paulos Mar Gregorios points out "Science is an activity that is taking place within God." In the words of Abraham Heschel, the famous Jewish philosopher,

> "*Science is unable to give all truth about all of our life. We are in need of the Spirit in order to know what to do with science. Science deals with relations among things within the universe; but man is endowed with the concern of the spirit and the spirit deals with the relation between the universe and God. Science seeks the truth about the universe; the spirit seeks the truth that is greater than the universe.*"[2]

Hence, both science and faith should be in the common pursuit of truth; they ought to be complementary.

What matters here is the public accountability of those who are engaged in the field of science and faith. The need of our times is a science and technology with a 'human face' that would contribute to the intrinsic values of life at all levels. In order to accomplish this, there should be a conscious negation of all idolatrous elements and forces of darkness in both areas and promotion of God given life in the community.

The exposition of this theme is within the basic theological framework that we have in the Bible, i.e., God-human-community-nature-Kingdom of God. Since it is beyond the scope of this study to go into all aspects of the theme, a reflection in the light of Mt. 24:3-14 would be appropriate.

1. What Did Jesus Say?

On two occasions, this question was posed to Jesus: Mt. 24:3-14 and Acts1: 6-11. Mt. 24:3-14.

> 3 *When he was sitting on the Mount of Olives, the disciples came to him*
> *privately, saying, "Tell us, when will this be, and what will be the sign of*
> *your coming and of the end of the age?"* 4 *Jesus answered them, "Beware*
> *that no one leads you astray.* 5 *For many will come in my name, saying, 'I*
> *am the Messiah!' and they will lead many astray.* 6 *And you will hear of*
> *wars and rumors of wars; see that you are not alarmed; for this must take*
> *place, but the end is not yet.* 7 *For nation will rise against nation, and*
> *kingdom against kingdom, and there will be famines and earthquakes in*
> *various places:* 8 *all this is but the beginning of the birth pangs.*

> [9] *"Then they will hand you over to be tortured and will put you to death, and you will be hated by all nations because of my name.* [10] *Then many will fall away, and they will betray one another and hate one another.* [11] *And many false prophets will arise and lead many astray.* [12] *And because of the increase of lawlessness, the love of many will grow cold.* [13] *But the one who endures to the end will be saved.* [14] *And this good news of the kingdom will be proclaimed throughout the world, as a testimony to all the nations; and then the end will come.*

Almost the same question is asked to the risen Jesus by his disciples in Acts 1:6-11.

> [6] *So when they had come together, they asked him, "Lord, is this the time when you will restore the kingdom to Israel?"* [7] *He replied, "It is not for you to know the times or periods that the Father has set by his own authority.* [8] *But you will receive power when the Holy Spirit has come upon you; and you will be my witnesses in Jerusalem, in all Judea and Samaria, and to the ends of the earth."* [9] *When he had said this, as they were watching, he was lifted up, and a cloud took him out of their sight.* [10] *While he was going and they were gazing up toward heaven, suddenly two men in white robes stood by them.* [11] *They said, "Men of Galilee, why do you stand looking up toward heaven? This Jesus, who has been taken up from you into heaven, will come in the same way as you saw him go into heaven."*

The first one was during the earthly ministry of Jesus and the second after his resurrection. Though a detailed exposition of these texts is beyond the scope of this section, what follows is a brief analysis of the texts.

a. The End is Unpredictable

In Peter's Pentecost message in Acts 2:17 this question comes to the fore. When the onlookers misunderstood the event of Pentecost, Peter gives an interpretation in the light of Joel 2:28-29. What does that mean? If the words of Peter were to be taken literally, then the end was on the day of Pentecost! As mentioned earlier, a literal interpretation would be counter productive here. Let us ponder on Matthew 24:3-14 little more deeply with regard to the meaning of the word "end."

> Jesus' words are quite clear; all end time predictions are either useless or hypocritical. Nevertheless, these abound in our spiritual world and people are after them. In our times such predictions go along with the contemporary market ideology, the make-it-easy Gospel and its 'prosperity doctrine.' High-tech media publicity and music are very often considered by many as the criteria of Christian spirituality! This author knows personally a few who left their homes and job 'to be with

the Lord' in his immanent coming! Some of these end time specialists and enthusiasts have disrupted family life and community life.

In Kerala, *Yuyomayam* was such a cult in the last century. Its leader claimed that he had some special revelation from God regarding the end times and he called people to be with him and wait for the Lord. When the 'appropriate time' came, the people asked, "Where is the Lord?" He said that the Lord came in the clouds, and only those who had special revelation could see it; and now the time of the millennium has already begun! Well, it's as if this cult almost had a natural death, perhaps with very few followers now. Jesus makes it clear that he himself is not aware of the end; it's left to the discretion of God the Father. Jesus also points out that the task of the church is to be in the process of witness with the power from above.

b. Issue of False Teachers

In a powerful article on "Beyond social distancing to fight COVID 19", Kalinga Tudor Silva shows how the pandemic spread became so severe in South Korea. According to him, it started with a Christian cult, known as the controversial Shincheonji Church of Jesus with a personality cult centered around an 88 year-old Lee Man-hee, who is self-identified as a messianic saviour. This cult facilitated the transmission of the disease from Wuhan to South Korea, because of the frequent travel among its followers. Consequently, more than half of all COVID19 patients in South Korea belonged to this sect.[3]

We have always had such cults and sects in the history of the church with varying degrees of truth claims and revelations. They are the representatives of the old, asserting themselves in the guise of the new. The true believers should have spirit of discernment here. The question is whether we have the preparedness to usher in the new. The issue of false teachers is expounded in 1 John 2:18-29. Here John summons his readers to be vigilant against the 'anti-Christ's, the enemies of Christ – those who are against the spirit of Christ, those who deny the Father and the Son. Here vs. 19 clearly points out that these people are the ones who left the church, perhaps in the context of persecution. One thing is to be noted here is that the enemies of the church are not necessarily those outside of us, they are from within – those who have no faith convictions in their life or those who would simply make a mockery of Christian faith. Another reference to anti-Christ is in Revelation13, which has to do with the idolatry of Rome.

Jesus' caution regarding the false teachers is as follows:

> [21] *"Not everyone who says to me, 'Lord, Lord,' will enter the kingdom of heaven, but only the one who does the will of my Father in heaven.* [22] *On that day many will say to me, 'Lord, Lord, did we not prophesy in your name, and cast out demons in your name, and do many deeds of power*

in your name?' [23] *Then I will declare to them, 'I never knew you; go away from me, you evildoers.'* – Mt. 7:21-23.

We have some guidelines as to how should we assess, a so-called spiritual programme.

- Does it preach the Gospel of the Kingdom of God as taught and lived by Christ?
- Is it miracle oriented or love oriented?
- Does it enable people to grow spiritually or does it make people submissive to the leaders?
- Do people really find answers to their emotional and social needs through such programmes?
- Is there a 'personality cult' in these programmes?
- Do these programmes lead people to Christ and His Kingdom and its values?

This is not to make value judgements on any particular group or church tradition. It also doesn't mean that in the main line churches everything is fine. Even today our life is in the midst of several idolatrous elements; the idolatry of religion, the idolatry of law, the idolatry of wealth, etc. An idol is that which blocks our ultimate loyalty to God.

c. Emergence of the New Involves Pain and Suffering

The term 'birth-pang' that is used in Matthew 24:8 denotes the emergence of the new. The same expression is found in Romans 8:22 which has to do with the "*groaning of the whole creation for renewal.*" Does it mean that wars, earthquakes and other natural calamities are bound to happen and those are the 'signs' of the return of Christ? A careful reading of the Biblical texts will reveal that the present order is not perfect and hence in the process of the ushering in of the new order struggles and pain are inevitable. We cannot equate this 'birth-pang' with any of the historical wars. Even though spiritual lessons can be drawn from natural calamities such as earthquakes and so on, such attitudes should not lead us to the naïve conclusion that before the return of the Lord the whole created order will be annihilated. Instead, studies by some of the environmental scientists have shown that human sin toward nature and the ruthless exploitation of the resources of the earth are some of the root causes of earthquakes and so on. The question here is whether we can become channels through which God's grace is poured into our midst. Here we are co-workers with God in the ushering in of the new.

d. The Proclamation of the Gospel of the Kingdom of God (vs.14)

The gospel of Jesus Christ is always the gospel of the Kingdom of God. The sure sign of the end is the proclamation of the Gospel of the Kingdom in the whole world and human response to it. In other words, the end is not a historical inevitability or progressive perfection of humanity as some of the secular ideologies point out. This is neither imposed on humanity from above nor the result of human struggles for justice and peace. Nevertheless, the Lord's coming and our becoming are deeply interwoven.

In the words of Leonardo Boff, "*The end is not a cosmic catastrophe but a consummation, an achievement of the end as the goal and fullness. What is already fermenting in creation will be fully realized.*" This new creation involves new values, new life style, new scale of loyalties, new concerns and new commitments.

The creation was cosmos out of chaos (order out of disorder). Ever since the creation of this world; the spirit has been active in the world. The incarnation of Christ is to be understood within the framework of the work of the Holy Spirit. The historical function of Christ was to redeem the created order from its aberrations. Rather than making end time calculations and predictions, the need of the times is our genuine response to historical events and promotion of the higher values of life.

5

Apocalyptic Writings
Daniel and Revelation

The book of Daniel and Revelation are the two apocalyptic books of the Bible. Both were written in the context of imperialism and persecution; Daniel in the context of the Babylonian Empire and Revelation in the context of the Roman Empire. Very little studies are done in this area in the main line church traditions. In the first part of this chapter, some of the issues in the interpretation of the apocalyptic literature are brought to the fore. The second part focuses on the main features of apocalyptic literature, with special reference to Revelation. Special attention is given to the anti-imperialistic agenda of both books. This challenges us to confront all imperial, hegemonic and fascist regimes in history.

Apocalypse is more often misunderstood than properly understood. It is very often associated with apocalyptic fantasies, truth claims, and hegemonic mindsets. Some of the Biblical literalists are stalwarts in this field, who with their individualistic visions and predictions threaten people with their truth claims! Whenever there is a war, a natural catastrophe, or a pandemic, the end time specialists would come up with the fulfilment of some of the apocalyptic passages. Hence, an in-depth approach regarding apocalyptic writings in general, and Biblical apocalyptic writings in particular, is essential. *Apocalupto* in Greek points to unveiling that which is hidden. We know God only to the extent to which he reveals himself to us. In Christian faith, God reveals in creation, in the person and work of Jesus Christ, in the life and ministry of the church. Bishop N. T. Wright gives a realistic definition of the apocalyptic.

> "*Apocalyptic was not a general principle about the way things happen in the world. It was the Biblical language to convey the meaning of one-off,*

> *unique event, the meaning of which belonged to its unique and disruptive role within the narrative of creation and covenant.*"[1]

He also points out that the apocalyptic uses the language of cosmic catastrophe to refer to actual political events.

Apocalyptic literature is broadly divided into two: Jewish apocalyptic literature and Christian apocalyptic literature. Both the Jewish and early Christian apocalyptic texts have a definite historical anchorage. In other words, they are not to be seen as vertical revelation from above without any horizontal connection. This gives us a hermeneutical tool in the interpretation of apocalyptic narratives that it should be historically rooted. As mentioned earlier, here let us remind ourselves that Christian faith is both historical as well as trans-historical.

The period of the apocalyptic literature is around the 3rd century BC to the 2nd century AD. This was mostly the period of the imperial regimes such as the Greek, Babylonian, Persian etc. The Jewish canonical apocalyptic books are Isaiah 24-27, 33-35; Jeremiah 33:14-26, Ezekiel 38-39, Joel 3:9-17, Zechariah 12-14, and Daniel 7-12. Besides these there are non-canonical books like Apocalypse of Adam, Apocalypse of Abraham, Greek apocalypse of Baruch, Syriac apocalypse of Baruch, Greek Apocalypse of Daniel, Apocalypse of Elijah, Apocalypse of Elijah, etc.

Daniel is considered as the last book written of the Old Testament. The present form of the book dates back to 2nd century BC. The author is considered as Daniel, who was an exile during the Babylonian regime. A few main theological thoughts of the book are given below.

One: Yahweh, the God of Israel, is the all-powerful King of all; even the gentile nations. People of God should give respect to the king; and also abide by the rules of the state so long as it won't lead to idolatry. They are summoned to worship only Yahweh. In the vision of Daniel, this is acknowledged, "*He changes times and seasons; he removes kings and sets up kings; he gives wisdom to the wise and knowledge to those who have understanding.*" – Dan. 2:21. In Daniel's interpretation of the King's dream, the divine commissioning of the King is acknowledged:*37 You, O king, the king of kings—to whom the God of heaven has given the kingdom, the power, the might, and the glory, 38 into whose hand he has given human beings, wherever they live, the wild animals of the field, and the birds of the air, and whom he has established as ruler over them all…*– Dan. 2:37-38.

According to some Biblical scholars, perhaps, Paul might have been influenced by this concept of the state when he says in Romans 13:1, "*Be subject to the Governing authorities; for there is no authority except from God.*"

Two: Kings of the world can become corrupt and absolutist in their authority. In such situations the Lord will intervene and establish His will (Daniel 4-5).

Three: All have to worship the living Lord. Even though they have to abide by the rules of the state, in case of a conflict, the primacy is the obedience to the will of God.

Four: When the kings assume the role of God, the faithful will have to protest (Dan. 3).

Five: The visions of Daniel are for the community, which point to the victory of God over the idolatrous powers.

Six: Eschatological thoughts – Dan. 7-12.The imperial rulers will be defeated by the God of heavens and the earth. The promises given to the king will be taken away in Dan. 5:18, "*O king, the Most High God gave your father Nebuchadnezzar kingship, greatness, glory, and majesty.*"

Daniel 12 gives a new insight in the entire Jewish tradition, which is considered as a reference to resurrection of the dead, eternal life, last judgment, and so on (vs.1-3). In other words, in the midst of despair and hopelessness, there are signs of hope and renewal.[2]

The main New Testament Apocalyptic narratives are Mt. 24, Mk. 13, 2 Thess. 2, and Revelation. The non-canonical New Testament writings are the *First Apocalypse of James, Second Apocalypse of James, Apocalypse of Paul, Apocalypse of Peter* and the *Apocalypse of Stephen*. Even though all these writings are significant, as mentioned earlier, this section only deals with the theological themes in the Canonical apocalyptic writings, with special reference to Daniel and Revelation.

The context of Apocalyptic writings is mainly that of persecution. For example, the book of Revelation was written in between 81-96 AD. According to New Testament scholars, this was the period of Emperor Domitian and the emperor cult was mandatory during this period. We have several references to the Emperor cult in the book. What we have in the New Testament is a Christian revision of the Jewish apocalyptic eschatology.

1. Issues in the Interpretation of Revelation

a. The Fall of the Empire

The collapse of the Roman empire was interpreted as the fulfilment of prophecy. With the conversion of Emperor Constantine, Christianity was made the official religion. Mainly through the Edict of Milan in 313 A.D, the Roman Empire became a so-called Christian Empire. Even though this period was initially considered as a blessed time for the church, eventually it was found by many in the church that Constantine's initiatives had only political considerations. Church history, especially the development of Christology, tells us that it was Constantine who convened the Nicene Council in 325 AD and his main concern was the homogenization of the Roman Empire as there were several divisive tendencies in the Empire, mainly due to the various Christological definitions. But the Roman Empire had a natural death in history and historians have divergent views on its downfall.[3] We can find traits of similar homogenizing tendencies in the present Indian governance; mainly under the Hindutva ideology. For example, imposition of Sanskrit in educational institutions, beef ban in some states in the North India, compulsory recitation of *Vandematharam* in schools, intolerance towards dissenting voices, and so on. Surprisingly, all these are under the guise of the Indian Constitution which is considered to be one of the most democratic constitutions in the world! Now efforts are under way in different parts of India, by the secular intellectuals and NGOs to read afresh the Preamble of the Constitution in public which clearly states that the State of India is Democratic, Secular, Socialist, and Pluralistic. While acknowledging the positive value of these attempts; we should not make any hasty conclusions, as the end time specialists very often do, that the end has come and the anti-Christs are in Delhi!

The notion here is that all fascist empires in history will have a natural death. Internal contradictions, political instability, economic depression, and crisis of leadership are very often pointed out as some of the reasons for the collapse of the Roman Empire. The details regarding the collapse are beyond the scope of this section.

b. World Negation and Otherworldly Interpretations

A clear dichotomy is made here between this world and the other world. The other world is real and the life in this world is only temporal and a preparation for the other world. Hence, any concrete involvement in history is considered futile. The task of the believers is only to get ready for the rapture and the second coming of the Lord. This attitude among the biblical literalists led to an escapist approach which is alien to the biblical truth.

c. Political

Scholars are of the view that in the political turmoil in the middle ages in Europe, Revelation had a definite impact. Some even interpreted that the prophecies in the book of Revelation were being fulfilled in the political history of Europe. This was some kind of a prediction–fulfilment approach. Some of the so-called spiritual leaders even started their own predictions along the lines of Revelation. This led to competitive truth claims.

d. War

Attempts were made to justify wars in the light of Revelation. For example, some saw the first World War as the beginning of the end times! It has been pointed out that during the first and second World Wars many in the West became super rich through the production and supply of food packets and medicine/hygiene kits in the refugee campuses. No wonder they would consider war as a blessing in disguise! Even now the so-called Bible-belt churches in U.S. and Europe are supportive of wars and they have Biblical justifications. But a careful reading of the down to earth realities would reveal that there is very little Biblical wisdom in this approach and what looms large is the market friendly prosperity doctrine.

e. Colonialism

Efforts were made to justify the colonial regimes in history in the light of the book of Revelation.[4] Thanks to the neo-colonial narratives and theological attempts.

2. Main Features of the Apocalyptic Literature with Special Reference to Revelation

a. Determinism

This is found mainly in the Jewish apocalyptic writings. Perhaps, this concept grew out of the exilic experiences and the long period of persecution of the believers. According to this thought, everything is pre-determined and God will do His mighty deeds in His own time (*kairos*). This doctrine is found in the Old Testament and the New testament, especially in the writings of St. Paul with special reference to Romans 8:28-29. In our times we have determinism in several spheres of life. Some of our economists point out that in the field of economics under globalization what looms large is 'economic determinism.' Political thinkers are talking about 'political determinism' and so on. The basic logic in all these is the same: Everything is determined; you just have to accept it and any attempt to change it will be futile. This has always been the logic of all imperial and oppressive regimes in history. Unfortunately, this was construed as the Biblical doctrine; the doctrine that supports the *status quo* and fascist powers in history. In the Kairos document of WCC, there is a chapter on the 'theology of the white church' which historically supported the apartheid regime in South Africa. Nevertheless, Nelson Mandela, Bishop Desmond Tutu, and the African National congress could challenge it in the light of Revelation 13. Here the faithful are challenged to fight against the idolatry of Rome which is symbolically portrayed as 666.

Two explanations can be given to the notion of determinism, especially in the Apocalyptic writings. First, the self-understanding of the persecuted community of faith. They might have received divine consolation through this approach. This faith gave them perseverance in the context of sufferings and also an awareness of God's decisive intervention in history. In other words, unlike some of the Greek concepts of God, who is beyond pain and suffering, in the book of Revelation, God is also affected by what happens on earth. Hence, the 'Slaughtered Lamb' is central theme of the book. Second, retrospective faith affirmation of the community. According to some of the New Testament writers, the entire narratives of the New Testament are retrospective faith affirmations of the early church. The attempt here is to view life and its realities from the perspective of faith. As mentioned earlier, this was mainly in the context of the suffering and persecution from Gentile emperors. In Daniel, Nebuchadnezzar is the oppressive emperor and in Revelation we have Domitian and others.

b Dualism

This is mainly due to Persian, Zoroastrian influence. In Zoroastrianism, there is always a fight between the good and evil. Zoroastrianism is very often considered as a monotheistic religion. The Zoroastrian god is called Ahura Mazda. It is a multi-tendency faith centered on a dualistic cosmology of good and evil, and an eschatology predicting the ultimate conquest of the evil. Ahura Mazda is the exalted, uncreated deity of wisdom in Zoroastrianism.[5] It served as the state religion of the Iranian empires and for more than a millennium and declined during the Muslim invasion of Persia in the 7th century AD. Even now, several Zoroastrians live in India, mainly in North India. Some Biblical scholars are of the view that in the cosmology of the apocalyptic writings, there is an influence of Zoroastrianism. It is beyond the scope of this section to go into a comparative study of the Zoroastrian and Apocalyptic texts.

Similarly, in the book of Revelation there is the dualism between this world and the other world, heaven and hell, holy and unholy, etc. This is also part of the Greek concept of the two-layered human person. For example, in Gnosticism, the human body is evil and the soul is immortal. Hence, the task of a human being is to negate the human body and to liberate the soul from the captivity of the body. This Gnostic heretical teaching is challenged in the Gospel of John when John presents Jesus as the incarnate one, "The Word became flesh and dwelt among us" (Jn.1:14) and also in the writings of Paul, "Therefore brethren, offer your bodies as a living sacrifice...(Rom.12:1). Through these, a spiritual significance is given to human body and bodily functions. Unfortunately, in the Christian doctrine of salvation over several centuries, cutting across church traditions, this dualism of the apocalyptic literature is dominant. For example, the common understanding of *soteria* is salvation from the world. Thanks to the contemporary developments in theology such as Eco-theology where salvation is considered in relation to creation and nature, and not away from nature. It is beyond the scope of this section to go into a detailed discussion on the doctrine of salvation.

c. Confrontationist Approach

The fight between God and Satan, between the saints and the wicked, good and evil, and light and darkness is an important theme in the apocalyptic writings, especially the book of Revelation. Even the concept of Satan is considered by many as an essential Christian doctrine. The question that Hans Kung raises sounds relevant here: Does God need an anti-God in order to be God?[6]

In a way, the apocalyptic narratives are polemical in nature. This approach has immense potentials provided this insight is seen as the basis to identify the historical forces of evil. But the Biblical literalists have very often made it as a justification for their 'hate campaign.' Even people of other faiths are considered by some as the enemies of God. Such leaders would always rule out any efforts to have dialogue with people of other faiths or ideologies on common issues of life.

This apocalyptic insight is very often used by Christian religious fundamentalists as a Biblical foundation for wars. Samuel T. Huntington's book, *The Clash of Civilization* points out that cultural wars are inevitable in the world.

d. Visions and Imageries

The U.S televangelist, Pat Robertson once claimed he had a vision that the so-called enemy of American capitalism, the President of Venezuela should be murdered! He even gave it as an advice to the President George Bush. But the worldwide media exposed the politics behind that vision and the President of U.S. also gave a deaf ear to that advice. Finally, Robertson said it was not a true vision from God! The *Left Behind* series by Tim Lahaye and Jerry B. Jenkins are considered as the final words in this area by some of the Christian dispensationalists.

Both the book of Daniel and Revelation are full of visions. Here a realistic understanding of the Biblical vision is essential. Here are a few thoughts along those lines.

One: Biblical vision is communitarian in nature. For example, the vision given to John in Patmos was not for himself, but for the persecuted church. Similarly, the vision of the burning bush given to Moses was for the community of Israel for their liberation.

Two: Biblical vision is either in crisis or leads to crisis. John was in crisis in Patmos and the vision was to see beyond that crisis. Daniel and his friends were in deep crisis and the visions were to empower them to stand for God and His Kingdom. The following words from Rabindranath Tagore, the famous Bengali poet in India are relevant here: All crisis situations are situations of grace. When you are in a crisis, the depth dimension of your life is revealed.

Three: Biblical vision is always for a mission. In other words, vision gives one a divine impatience to come out of the comfort zones and to stand for truth and values. This may be an invitation to give up one's narrow domestic or individualistic dreams. The visions given to Joseph, Mary, Saul, Peter, and John in Patmos are all examples.

e. Anti-imperialistic Notion

In the book of Daniel, we have the negation of Babylonian imperialism and in Revelation the negation of Roman imperialism. All imperial regimes in history have been hegemonic and oppressive. The colonial era witnessed the imperialism of the West which was marked by conquests, occupations, and subjugations. Colonialism was certainly dependent upon the use of force and physical coercion .An important post-colonial task is to challenge the prevailing hegemonic assumptions, deterministic attitudes, and to participate in 'decolonizing the mind' at all levels. But, changing the mindset is not an easy task.

Ania Loomba sets the tone for post-colonial thinking in the following words: *The process of forming a community in the new land necessarily meant unforming or reforming the communities that existed there already and involved a wide range of practices including trade, plunder, negotiation, warfare, genocide, enslavement, and rebellions.*[7]

The postcolonial narratives, on the whole, try to decolonize the enslaving myths, ideologies, and legacy of the colonial era. This is a process of disengagement from the whole colonial enterprise. The study of religious myths in the 19th century was mainly an attempt to reinforce the cultural hegemony of the West. As Kwok Pui-Lan observes,

> *The study of the Buddhist and Hindu classical texts created the myth that the East was static, unchanging, and that its glory was long gone, surpassed by the vitality and progress of the Christian West. In the 19th century Europe it was commonly believed that the world's population existed as a hierarchy of 'races' based upon colour, with white Europeans deemed the most civilized and the black Africans as the most savage.*[8]

Though the latter half of the 20th century witnessed the independence of several countries, the mindset of the colonized did not undergo much change. This is the context of the search for a "postcolonial subjectivity" which consists of the colonizer, the colonized, and the collaborators. The colonized nations' religion, culture, myths and symbols were construed as backward and hence they had to be replaced by the colonizers' superior religion and culture! By highlighting this complexity of imperialism, the postcolonial theories generally point out that it is something more than a foreign rule of one nation by another and the colonial mindset and conditioning continues for generations even after the collapse of the colonial rule.

While sternly questioning all the Western, colonial attempts to give divine sanctions to imperialistic trends, M. M. Thomas attempts a Christological interpretation of the Asian revolution. In his system, the purpose of theology is

> *...not to find divine sanction for historical movements, but to help discern what is of Christ and what of the devil in that movement so that we may know the nature of our response of faith. True theology is not a means of enhancing self-righteousness and political messianism; but a spiritual response of constructive and discriminating participation.*[9]

In India, even several decades after the colonial period, we are yet to affirm our identity as an Indian church. Even the St.Thomas Christians are struggling hard to define and affirm their Syrian-ness and not Indian-ness! Our identity as a community of faith ought to be in relation to and not over against those who are in search for human dignity and fullness of life.

After the neo-Hindu reformers, we have very few voices in the field of Indian Christian Theology. Are we still post-colonial or still colonial? For most of our theological studies, we are heavily dependent on the West. Interestingly, even for post-colonial studies we depend mostly on Western literature! When are we going to be liberated from this theological imperialism?

This is not to underestimate or totally negate the contributions of the West to the historical development of theology. Even among the missionaries in India, we have had the agents of British East India Company as well as social reformers. Some of them have made significant contributions to the field of education, medical field, literature, and so on.

f. Negation of Idolatry

An 'idol' is that which blocks our ultimate loyalty to God and our search for an authentic life in the community. It is giving ultimate loyalty to that which is penultimate. There are both religious idols and secular idols. It can be a personified evil, system, institution, or socio-political models which would demand blind worship and absolute obedience. In a way, all imperial regimes in history have been idolatrous. Such idols are mentioned in the book of Daniel and Revelation. This is mostly the idolatry of the state such as the imperial cult and idolatry of power, etc. They always denied human rights, religious freedom, and community life. They never tolerated dissenting voices. Idols of death such as the idolatry of power, idolatry of wealth, idolatry of caste, etc are found in all communities. In any attempt to transform the local situations, these idolatrous elements are to be confronted with the power of the risen Christ. Our task here is to manifest Jesus Christ as the Lord of life over against all powers of death at all levels. This is possible only through our partnership with all those who are allies of the higher values of life at all levels.

Revelation makes a distinction between the seal (mark) of the beast and the mark of the Lamb (Rev. 13:15-17). Biblical scholars point out that in the Roman Empire it was a common practice of the slave masters to put a mark on the body of their slaves to identify them. It is also said that some of the cruel masters used to burn the bodies of their slaves to make the marks more evident. In the liturgical theology of the Eastern Church tradition, this metaphor is used in the Order of Baptism.

After the naming ceremony of the child, the celebrant says, "*O Lord God, cast out all the wicked dealings of the Evil One from this your creation and handiwork, who has been sealed in your name. Rebuke the rebellious traitor. Cleanse him/her from the spirit of deceit. May he/she not be the dwelling place of Satan...but the sanctuary of God.*"[10]

The confession of the Lordship of Christ and the negation of idolatry are heavily interwoven. This was in the context of socio-economic ideology, political imperialism, and the idolatry of the state of Rome. Pablo Richard enables us to see the question of idolatry in a new perspective. Reflecting on the Latin American context of marginalization, he points out that the central issue is not atheism but idolatry–worship of false gods of a system of oppression and idols that sanction anti-life forces. In a discussion on the Biblical theology of confrontation with idolatry, especially in the context of Rev. 13, he delineates how for the early Christians the Lordship of Christ was incompatible with the worship of the beast and its idol. It was in this sensitive context that Jesus Christ was confessed as the only Lord (a dangerous confession indeed); entailing a radical de-idolization of the Roman Empire that is reduced to the condition of a 'beast.'

According to him, "*...the de-idolization of the Roman Emperor entailed the negation of the whole divinized transcendent and supernatural world created by the Roman Empire, with all its promises of liberation and its religious values touching on human life and culture.*"[11]

This enables us to identify some of the contemporary idols – the ideological weapons of death – in our socio-political, economic, and religio-cultural areas. Hence, a critique of 'idolatry' in this sense is essential in our Christological articulation; critiques in terms of ultimate values such as love, justice, life, and so on. As Christians should not fall into the trap of making an idolatry of the Lordship of Jesus or 'Christodolatry'[12] which would only result in tragic ethical consequences in the community life. Our Christological task in a postcolonial context is to identify and challenge the notions of idolatry in all traditions, including the Christian faith; the idolatry of caste, the idolatry of wealth (mammon), the idolatry of power, the idolatry of state, the idolatry of technology, and so on. Therefore, the proclamation of the Lordship of Christ in reality is not to consecrate these idolatrous elements but to confront and struggle against them along with all others in our common pilgrimage of faith.

Luna Dingayam, a Filipino theologian, suggests "*a conversion in our Christological articulation.*" The concern here is to bring out a "people's Christology" in the context of people's struggles in the Philippines. Dingayam considers people as the judging criterion in Christological reflections:

> *Christologies can be true or false in terms of how they are being appropriated for the people. A Christology is false if and when it is used by the powers-that-be to exercise control and dominance over the suffering people in a given historical moment.... And a Christology is true when it is of service to the people – one that would lead them to a deeper understanding of their task as God's people in the world.*[13]

The implication is that the Christian witness to Jesus as the Lord should not be a threatening claim for those who belong to other traditions as they may not make the same witness as we do in the light of our faith tradition.

An attempt is also made to find an essential link between the proclamation of Jesus concerning the kingdom of God and the confession of Jesus as the Lord. The Kingdom and the living Lord were proclaimed as two related entities. The *Kyrios* Christology was not separate from the Kingdom concept. Even though the *Kyrios* became the dominating idea regarding Christ's status, this title did not get its context only from Hellenistic *Kyrios* ideologies, but to a great extent from Kingdom ideas.[14]

The postcolonial context is not a monolith in terms of culture, politics, or ideology. In other words, the realities in postcolonial contexts are different. Colonialism has functioned in subtle ways in the colonized nations. There was a time when the Western theology was considered as the 'manual or universal theology' and the Asian and Indian as 'optional or contextual theology.' Christian theology, especially Christology was even used as an ideological weapon by the colonizers for their hegemonic designs. Hence, several of the exclusivist and absolutistic claims are re-examined in postcolonial contexts, both in religious and secular spheres. Today, there is a growing awareness that we must be on our guard against all notions of authority. Gone are the days of pyramidical and hierarchical authority. The Lordship of Christ should not be equated with those forms of authority which people reject in their search for freedom and selfhood. authority should be justified only if it has the potentials for the common good and impetus for human progress towards perfection.

One of the concerns of this section has been to make sense out of the apocalyptic tradition highlighting some of its salient features and also critiquing the otherworldly approach of the dispensationalists. As mentioned earlier, the author has not gone into a detailed Biblical exegesis of the apocalyptical narratives. The focus was more on the thematic understanding of the narratives.

One of the questions that often comes to the fore is the relationship as well as the distinction between the apocalyptic tradition and the prophetic tradition. Before going any further, a few words about both these traditions are timely:

Prophetic tradition is a continuation and transformation of the present. What matters here is the historical obedience to God as concrete historical human beings. The prophets emphasized obedience to God through the covenant, repentance, and the need to turn to God and to promote justice and righteousness. The apocalyptic focuses on conflict with the present systems; patience and perseverance in sufferings.

Here it is to be acknowledged that the Bible has both these traditions. In the life and ministry of Jesus also we see both. But, overall, Jesus mostly was within the prophetic tradition. Though there are a few apocalyptic imageries in his discourses such as the "son of man coming in glory" passages, etc., he always quoted from the prophetic writings. The servant of Yahweh concept of the Old Testament, especially in what are known as the "*servant songs*" (Isa. 42:1-9; 49:1-6; 50:4-11; 52:13-54:12) was taken over by the Gospel writers to interpret the person and work of Christ. The self-understanding of Jesus was that he was the suffering servant of Yahweh who was sent on a particular historical mission (Mk. 10:45, Lk. 4:18ff).Christian churches down the ages have interpreted Jesus as the one who embodied the suffering servant passages in Isaiah and also the 'lion of Judah' who is strong enough to open the seal.

g. The Ultimate Victory of God and the Victims

This has to do with the triumph of God over the forces of evil structures. In the miraculous deliverance of Daniel and his friends from the lions' den and on several occasions in Revelation we have this theme. A brief survey of the Christological themes in Revelation would be helpful here:

i. The Lamb Slaughtered (Rev. 5:6-10)

What comes to the fore is the theology of the cross. As mentioned earlier, rather than giving ritualistic or magical powers to the 'bleeding face of Jesus' as was the norm during the middle ages, what is more important is our life on the way of the cross. In other words, there is an inevitability of the cross in the life of Jesus and also in our life. The task here is to take up his cross and follow him (Mk. 8:34). This will definitely have consequences in our personal and social life. I think we have a definition of the church here: Christians are followers of Jesus on the way of the cross unto its fulfilment. In other words, church membership should be evaluated in the light of our proximity to the way of the cross and its credible manifestation not counting the cost.

In history we have examples of leaders using this method in their movements. For example, in India, Mahatma Gandhi admits that his *ahimsa* was inspired by the cross of Christ. This was the weapon that he used against the imperial British for the Indian independence. Similarly, Martin Luther King Jr. used this method in his liberation movement of the Blacks in U.S. and Nelson Mandela in his fight against apartheid in South Africa.

ii. The Power of the Lamb

This may sound like a contradiction. As we are aware, the wild animals like lion, tiger and leopard are considered as the animals with muscle power. The animal planet channels continuously show how they dominate their prey. Nevertheless, this apocalyptic symbolism has immense potentials in our life of faith. The power of the lamb is the power of the cross; it is the power of love and not the love for power. "*The Lamb is an amazing and yet wonderfully disarming vision in the face of Rome's ideology of Victory; the victorious Lamb of Revelation looks almost incongruous.*"[15] This is to be seen within the framework of the servant Lamb of Isaiah 53. Here is a reversal of the power of lion with that of the lamb. "*Then I saw between the throne and the four living creatures and among the elders a Lamb, appeared to have been killed*" (Rev. 5:6). This power of love which the Lamb theology manifests is totally ignored by the dispensationalists and the crusaders who threaten people with certain apocalyptic imageries. The power of the Lamb is the power of witness, the power of love, and solidarity with the victims of oppression and not necessarily the power of military might.

iii. Jesus Christ the Lord of History

The terms 'Lord' or 'Lordship' are definitely open to several misunderstandings. In many circles, it is equated with the autocratic power of monarchs demanding blind obedience and thereby suppressing human freedom and dignity. Lordship, kingship, and *status quo* are often mentioned in the same breath. Some even hold that this title has become outdated and obsolete in contemporary times. There are several thinkers who find only feudal and imperialistic overtones in the expression 'the Lordship of Christ.'

It is understandable that in our age of democracy and freedom, any kind of Lordship category is naturally taken with an element of suspicion and even as an assault on human freedom and selfhood. While affirming some of the negative connotations of the category, since the confession "Jesus is Lord" was one of the hallmarks of the early Christian tradition and continues as an important area of Christian witness today, the basic focus here is to search for new and positive implications of this category. In a situation of pluralism, what is more desirable is to underscore this servant image of Jesus Christ which will always enable us to re-examine our culturally biased concepts of Lordship. Some of the main dimensions of the servant Lord are the following:

One: The pattern of the Servant Lord

Some of the Asian thinkers have wondered whether the 'servant image' would further lead to the justification of the unjust socio-economic systems: e.g. slavery, racism, male chauvinism, etc. However, Hyun Kyung, a Korean feminist, finds liberative elements in this image. She considers the servant image of Christ as a meaningful category in the struggle of Asian women for freedom and selfhood. While drawing attention to several 'Lord images' in Asia, which are products of the colonial and patriarchal system, she says:

> *If the liberative dimension of the suffering servant image frees Asian women from imposed suffering as a consequence of their own choice for liberation, the liberative dimension of the Lord image of Jesus frees Asian women from false authority of the world over them and empowers them to claim the authority which springs from life-giving experiences.*[16]

In other words, the servant-Lord image offers us a critique of all forms of arbitrary, oppressive, and patriarchal lordships and enables us to say no to domination and subjugation. Hence, this servant image does not give any one the 'divine sanction' to justify any of the socio-political models, systems or institutions. Jesus' dominion and authority are in no way similar to those of world rulers. He dominates through God's pain-love, service, and sacrifice.

Two: Reversal of the concept of Lordship

In Jesus Christ, the servant-Lord we are confronted with a reversal of values. The famous Christological hymn in Philippians 2:5-10 draws our attention as to how the servanthood of Christ is related to his Lordship. The key terms here are '*emptied himself*', '*took the form of a servant*', '*humbled himself*', and '*became obedient unto death.*' All these values are to be cherished in our understanding of the Lordship of Jesus Christ. The letter to the Hebrews too spells it out in a clear manner: He was made completely like us, capable of feeling our weakness with us, put to test in exactly the same way as ourselves...and made perfect through pain (Heb. 2:10-18; 4:15; 5:7-10). He is the Lord not because of his power to rule over others but because he is the one who was despised, rejected, spat upon, and killed like a criminal outside the walls (Heb. 13:12). Therefore, his servanthood, vulnerability, and humiliation are the hallmarks of his Lordship in the book of Revelation. "*Then the seventh angel blew his trumpet, and there were loud voices in heaven, saying: The power to rule over the world belongs now to our Lord and His Messiah, and He will rule for ever and ever*" (Rev. 11:15).

This Lordship is not to be identified with that of a tyrant but in terms of the suffering servant; not in terms of domination and privilege but in terms of the service and sacrifice. In Matthew 20:25-27 and Mark 10:43-44, we find Jesus sternly refusing any attempt to lord over others. He also enables us to define authority and lordship in terms of suffering as a slave through the symbolic act of washing the disciples' feet (Jn.13:12-17). We have here a clear negation of all arrogant and triumphalist attitudes. This reversal of the concept of Lordship in terms of service and sacrifice must commend itself in the situation of pluralism in Asia.

h. Jesus Christ the King of Kings

Daniel 7:13-14 talks about the everlasting authority of the 'son of man.'

> *I saw what looked like a son of man. He was approaching me, surrounded by clouds and he went to the one who had been living for ever and was presented to him. He was given authority, honour and royal power so that the people of all nations, races and languages would serve him. His authority would last for ever."*

In Revelation we see Jesus is presented as a warrior riding on a white horse and defeating the satanic forces.

> *"Then I saw heaven open, and there was a white horse. Its rider is called the Faithful and the True; it is with justice that he judges and fights his battles. His eyes were like a flaming fire and he wore many crowns on his head. He had a name written on him but no one except himself knows what it is. The robe he wore was covered with blood. His name is the "Word of God." The armies of heaven followed him, riding on white horses and dressed in clean white linen. Out of his mouth came a sharp sword, with which he will defeat the nations. He will rule over them with a rod of iron and he will trample out the wine in the winepress of the furious*

> *anger of the Almighty God. On his robe and on his thigh was written the name: "King of Kings and lord of lords"* (Rev.19:11-21).

The Christological symbols and war imageries in the text deserve special attention. A few ethical questions come to the fore in this context are the following:

- Is there a holy war?
- Can we use violence to overcome violence?
- Do we need to present Jesus as a crusader as it was done during the Middle Ages?
- Who are the enemies of the church in our times – are they within our traditions or outside?

Well, here it is to be admitted that Jesus Christ is the King with a difference. He is the righteous King who demands justice and righteousness from us. When the people of Israel demanded a King like those in the neighbouring nations, they were questioning the sovereignty of God (Theocracy). Nevertheless, God asks Samuel to anoint a king for them. In the installation ceremony, a clear divine mandate is given so that the kingship in Israel would emulate the values of the justice and righteousness (1 Sam10:17-26). But the history of Israel tells us that kingship in Israel was a failure, even though there were a few exceptions. Hence, the prophetic oracles regarding the coming of a righteous king. This King will not give anyone the license to absolutely rule over others in His name. Revelation's wake-up call to be with God in Christ in the ushering in of the new should be at the centre of Christian life and ministry.

i. Inclusiveness of Heaven

In chapter 7 of Revelation we have this vision. In the first part of this text, the entry into heaven is for the representatives of the twelve tribes of Israel; afterwards, we see a great multitude.

> "*After this I looked and there was an enormous crowd –no one could count all the people! They were from every race, tribe, nation and language and they stood in front of the throne and of the Lamb, dressed in white robes and holding palm branches in their hands. They called out in a loud voice: Salvation comes from our God who sits at the throne and from the Lamb!...He said to me, these are the people who have come safely through the terrible persecution. They have washed their robes and made them white with the blood of the Lamb*" (Rev7:9-14).

Our usual understanding of heaven is turned upside down here. In Christian spirituality, heaven is an exclusive place that is reserved for the righteous. The common spiritual goal is very often considered as a place of safety and security here and a safe place in heaven after death. As pointed out earlier, the criterion to enter heaven is our life on the way of the cross and the willingness to bear its consequences. The text also points out that the blood that is shed for the Gospel of the Kingdom will not be a waste.

The Christian concept of heaven has been criticized by many in history. The sharpest among them would be the one by Karl Marx. He found an unholy alliance among the feudal lords, capitalists, and the priests. This was mainly in the context of European Christianity of his times. In his sharp critique on Religion, especially Christian faith, he wrote:

> "*The classical saint of Christianity mortified his body for the salvation of the souls of the masses; the modern, educated saint mortifies the bodies of the masses for the salvation of his own soul.*"[17]

Well, instead of being defensive, the content of these words is to be given due attention. Some observations are in place:

- Does the Christian, in our concept of heaven, justify unjust socio-political structures and systems?
- Can the church effectively participate in social struggles with ultimate concerns?
- How do we explain the church's unholy alliance with the oppressive regimes in history?
- In our concept of salvation can we go beyond the 'salvation of the souls' and 'security in heaven'?

In our attempt to reinterpret heaven, eternal life, and so on; an insight from Revelation would be helpful:

> "*And I saw the Holy City, New Jerusalem coming down out of heaven from God, prepared and ready, like a bride ready to meet her husband. I heard a loud voice speaking from the throne. Now God's home is with humankind! He will live with them and they shall be his people*" (Rev. 21:2-4).

This is a down-to-earth description of heaven. Hans-Ruedi Weber's words are significant in this context:

> *Christians and Christian movements are tempted to narrow down the cosmic hope of the Biblical faith. With false humility they often romanticize weakness and poverty. Such an attitude can lead to a mediocre piety: the hope for the universe becomes then a privatized religion of saved souls while the Caesars of this world remain unchallenged.*[18]

As mentioned earlier, here the faithful are not taken up to heaven; rather heaven is coming down. If so, our task is not to romanticize heavenly bliss but to make earthly life more meaningful, God centered, and justice oriented. In other words, heaven is not to be construed as a place to go after our life on earth, but a state of life where peace, justice, and righteousness will flourish.

6

The Kingdom of God

The Kingdom God was the main concern and vision of Jesus. He taught the Kingdom and manifested the Kingdom and its values. He was always a prophet of the *escaton,* a harbinger of hope for all. He always challenged those forces which were against the Kingdom; the forces of sin, patriarchy, religious hierarchy and political authority. In the life and ministry of Jesus, we have a blending of both the prophetic and mystic dimensions of spirituality. Any attempt to interpret the Kingdom without the mindset and the perspectives of Jesus would be defective. In other words, we cannot preach Jesus without the Kingdom of God. The task of the Church is to promote a spirituality that is conducive to the furtherance of the Kingdom dimension in our times. But, the Church has historically deviated from this central vision of Jesus.

All his teachings were based on the Kingdom of God and all his deeds were manifestations of the Kingdom. His attempts to manifest the Kingdom through his healings, especially on Sabbath; his Sermon on the Mount, which is considered as the ethics of the Kingdom–all these had dire consequences in his ministry. Rather than making the truth claims that the church is the sign and sacrament of the Kingdom; the task of the church is to discern the signs of the Kingdom in our times. Such signs can be seen within and outside the church.

1. The Values of the Kingdom of God

Peace, justice, and righteousness are the main values of the Kingdom. The peace that Jesus gives is not *pax romana,* (Roman peace)or in contemporary terms, peace at gun point.

The relationship between legal justice and redemptive justice is also significant. The Psalmist says, "*steadfast love and faithfulness meet; righteousness and peace kiss each other.*" (Ps. 85:10) M. M. Thomas reminds us that our struggle for legal justice and our stances for redemptive justice which transcends legal justice would bring in sufferings for the church.

A distinction has to be made between legal and redemptive justice. Legal justice, though important, has its limitations, because legal justice is through the judicial system. Very often we say: All are equal before the law! But some of the stalwarts in the Judicial field in India, like Justice Krishna Iyer, Kurien Joseph, and others have pointed out that even within the Indian Judicial system, justice is very often a distant dream for the poor and marginalized.While underscoring the efforts to achieve justice, Emilio Castro, the former General Secretary of WCC, brings out its Biblical dimension as follows:

> *Justice is the response demanded from those who listen to the call of the Kingdom, it is a penultimate goal, paving the way for the actualization of the Kingdom of God in history. Justice in its biblical sense is rehabilitating justice. It is not to give one what he or she deserves; it is to provide everyone what he or she needs to enter into the dynamics of the Kingdom.*[1]

Jesus wants His followers to promote peace, justice, and righteousness at all levels. The emergence of the new would always bring sufferings and pain. Jesus says, "*Blessed are the peacemakers.*" He doesn't say, blessed are the peace lovers or those who believe in peace! In other words, peace-making should be seen as a task that is given to us. The risen Jesus also blesses his disciples in a similar manner. "*Eight days later, his disciples were inside again, and Thomas was with them. Jesus came and stood among them and said: 'Peace be with you.'*" (Jn. 20:26). This portion is traditionally understood as the restoration of Thomas; because here Jesus shows him his hands with the marks of the nail. But, rather than the restoration of Thomas from his disbelief; this should be seen as the commissioning of the disciples for the mission of God's *shalom*. This is because the risen Jesus is counting on them.

In Romans 17, Paul reminds us that the main values of the Kingdom of God are peace, righteousness, and joy in the Holy Spirit (Rom.14:17). The Hebrew word used for peace here is *shalom,* which is translated as the state of good relationships in the community, wellness of all etc. This is not the peace of the graveyard; it's not a shallow peace. This peace cannot be built on the foundations of injustice. Rather than an inner consolation which is the result of our devotion to Jesus, *shalom* is peace in the community, peace in our relationships. As Paul reminds us, this is inevitably on the way of the cross. "He is our peace; He has broken down the walls of partition" (Eph. 2:14-15). Jesus wants us to be peace makers and not simply peace lovers.

2. Spirituality of the Kingdom

Recall that Christian spirituality is very often understood as a life of safety and security here and a safe place in heaven in most of the spiritual circles. It seems that the Gnostic spirituality of the early centuries is what looms large in the Christian spirituality. The Gnostics saw everything in dualistic terms; the spirit and matter, body and soul, earthly and heavenly, divine and human and so on. Some of the Gnostic teachers even advocated that the human body is the seat of all evil and hence the spirituals should deny their body for the immortality of their souls. Salvation for them was the liberation of the soul from the captivity of the body. Such a dichotomy is alien to the Gospel of Christ. Hence, the 'incarnational dimension'is at the core of a genuine Christian spirituality. What comes to the fore here is God's pain-love (agape) (Jn. 3:16). The way Christ confronts the realities of human life such as sickness, bereavement, demon possession, poverty, male chauvinism, and legalism are all examples of this new pattern of spirituality Christ has set before us.

The best framework in our search for alternatives and the higher values of life is the Kingdom of God which was the central vision of Jesus. He always taught and lived the Kingdom. All his miracles or signs were really manifestations of the Kingdom. Jesus lived with the vision that the Kingdom would one day be a reality on earth. Christian gospel is essentially the Gospel of the Kingdom of God. Rather than a place to go after one's death which is unrelated to life on earth, the Kingdom is to be understood as the ultimate state of perfection, a life with God in its fullness.

We need a conceptual clarification here by negating two notions. First, that spirituality relates only with the individual soul. Secondly, that spirituality is over against life in this world and its realities. This calls for a brief explanation. Bishop John A. T. Robinson who is known for his critical stances in theology, points out that the presence of God is to be sought in the world and not away from the world. God is not "up there" in the heavens but "down here" on earth. In other words, Christian spirituality is not merely the spirituality of an isolated soul but the spirituality of the human being in relationship with God, with other human beings, and with nature. This spirituality is inevitably in the community. This is a Christian faith response to life which includes both a vision and praxis. Let us also acknowledge that there are various faith responses in other religious traditions and secular notions in secular and agnostic ideologies.

3. Prophetic Spirituality and Mystic Spirituality

Prophetic spirituality is found mostly in three major prophetic religions: Judaism, Christianity, and Islam. It is beyond the scope of this chapter to go into the details here. *Prophetic* here means prophetic obedience to God as concrete historical human beings. God-human-world-Kingdom is the framework that we have in Christian faith. The main mystic religions are Hinduism, Buddhism, and Jainism. In the ministry of Jesus, there is a blending of both the prophetic and mystic dimensions. The best example is the Mount of Transfiguration. Jesus took Peter, James, and John with him. The discussion on the summit was concerning his suffering and death in Jerusalem. In other words, this can be considered as a 'mystic experience' of Jesus. Moses and Elijah's appearance in the clouds is to strengthen him on the way of the cross. To put it differently, within the mystic experience, the prophetic tradition comes to the fore. Immediately after the vision, Jesus goes down to the valley; the 'valley of disfiguration.' As soon as they are in the valley, Jesus and his disciples were confronted with the bare realities of life; the boy with an unclean spirit and so on! The focus is that Christian life is always on the way of the cross. It is a journey from the 'Mount of Transfiguration' (our contemplation, prayer life, etc) to the 'valley of disfiguration' (the field of concrete actions). Jesus' prayer is not to avoid the cross, but to strengthen him to face it (Lk. 9:28-43).

4. Kingdom Perspective on Life

The Kingdom of God gives us a new perspective on life: that life on earth is God's gift and our task is to make it accountable and sacred. Kingdom also challenges us to do away with all preoccupations with our mundane existence. Here is an invitation to see the beyond dimension of life and affirm the sanctity and sacredness of life. Emilio Castro writes,

> *"The Kingdom of God is an invitation to see beyond the present realities, the power of the age to come, and to find in that power the inspiration to confront the actual historical ambiguities. God calls people to go forward, to look for the new land, for the new justice."*[2]

The Biblical concept of the Kingdom is both a view of life (*darsana*-vision) and way of life (*dharma*-ethics). An integral relationship between these two insights is essential in our understanding of the Kingdom.

In Christian spiritual circles, very often, two notions of the Kingdom are evident: Christ without the Kingdom (in extreme evangelical piety) and Kingdom without Christ (in radical action groups). Both these are defective approaches. In one of the reports of the Melbourne Conference of W.C.C which met under the theme Thy Kingdom Come said, "This prayer comforts us and it also disturbs us."

5. Two Dimensions of the Kingdom

Jesus gives us two dimensions of the Kingdom: the present and futuristic. He says, "The Kingdom is in your midst" and he exhorts us to pray, "Thy Kingdom come." In other words, the Kingdom has already come; nevertheless, its culmination is yet to come. Hence our life is in between these two realities – the 'already'and the 'not yet'of the Kingdom of God. As S. Kappen points out:

> *It is the future that is already breaking in upon the present.... The tension between the 'already' and 'not yet' must be maintained at any cost. He gives two reasons in this regard:*

One-All authentic human existence is marked by the tension between faith in the present and hope for the future. According to him, commitment to any cause would be half-hearted if it is devoid of a commitment to an absolute cause.

Two: If the 'already' and 'not yet' dimension is ignored, we shall run the risk of making idols of our past as well as present achievements, and refusing to march forward to God, who beckons us from the beyond.[3]

This means that the growth of the Kingdom is inevitably in and through our life; through the realities, uncertainties, and predicaments of history. Hence, our task is not simply to wait and see how God will establish His Kingdom but to be with God in the concrete realities of history so that the Kingdom would be manifested into reality. This dialectic of the Kingdom, the 'already' and the 'not yet', should be given due attention in our understanding of the concept of the Kingdom as manifested by Jesus. In Jesus' teachings, the present involves the future and vice versa.

Nevertheless, we should do away with two wrong notions here:

One: The Kingdom is something that God is going to establish in the future without human participation. This assumes that the Kingdom is the destined future no matter what human beings do on earth. This ahistorical approach is found in several of the Christian church traditions.

Two: The Kingdom as a human construct through the historical struggles for justice and human rights. This notion was evident in the Social Gospel movement in U.S in the last century. But, several of them took a back seat with the collapse of Communism in Eastern Europe. Even this author can think of two student movements which were active in college campuses in India: the Student Christian Movement and the Evangelical Union. The former one was mostly inspired by the radical interpretation of the Gospel, especially Liberation Theology, social action programmes, etc. And the latter focused on the literal interpretation of the Gospel with pietistic lifestyle, personal salvation, etc. In a way, from a theological perspective, the former emphasized the present dimension of the Kingdom of God and the latter emphasized the futuristic dimension of the Kingdom. But to put it bluntly, both have misunderstood the Gospel of the Kingdom of God as taught and lived by Christ.

6. The Question of Values

A genuine quest for value is one of the signs of an authentic community. There are two types of values: instrumental and intrinsic. The instrumental value has to do with our biological existence; the things that we possess, our family identity, our social positions, power, community status, etc. The intrinsic value has to do with the higher realms of life, such as our commitment, Christian influence in a particular context, concrete stances for the values of the Kingdom of God, etc. Unfortunately, our media, both print and electronic, is obsessed with the instrumental value of life. It seems as if that which is not saleable or marketable is of no value at all! There is always a tension between the values of the market such as competition, success, profit, etc and the values of the Kingdom such as love, compassion, justice, fellowship, etc. Here is the cutting edge of the Gospel: "You cannot serve both God and mammon" (Mt 6:24). As pointed out earlier, the choice here is between the idols of death and the God of life.

7. Conversion to the Kingdom

The challenge of Jesus is "The time is fulfilled, and the Kingdom of God has come near; repent, and believe in the good news." (Mk.1:15) Our concern for value has to be measured in terms of our proximity to the Kingdom and its righteousness (Mt 6:33).Conversion is not necessarily from other religions to Christian faith even though such instances are bound to happen out of human inner compulsions. Genuine conversion is to the Kingdom of God and its righteousness. The challenge here is to say yes to the values of the Kingdom and no the values of the market. So, there ought to be a continuous 'conversion of the converted' with in the church.

On the question of the political significance of this conversion and also the political dimension of the Kingdom, Leonardo Boff, highlights the need to understand the life and mission of Jesus in its entirety:

> *He is indeed the Messiah-Christ, but not one of a political nature. His Kingdom cannot be particularized, and reduced to a part of reality, such as politics. He came to heal all reality in all its dimensions, cosmic, human and social. The great drama of the life of Christ was to try to take the ideological content out of the word, "Kingdom of God" and to make the people and his disciples comprehend that he signified something much more profound, namely that he demands a conversion and a radical transformation of the human world; the he demands a love of the friends and enemies alike, and the overcoming of all elements inimical to God and humankind.*[4]

In other words, all of us stand in need of a genuine conversion in our life: conversion from sin to God, from pride to humility, from accumulation to sharing, from death to life. Rather than making exclusive truth claims about ourselves, the need of the times is to vindicate the claims that we make. Let us honestly admit that we have not yet become what we ought to become in Christ. We are all Christians in the making, and the best is yet to be.

8. The Spirituality of Jesus

The spirituality of Jesus was always within the prophetic tradition. There is a synthesis of contemplation and combat in his spirituality. The best Biblical example is the 'Mount of Transfiguration' which can be considered as his vision or a mystic experience. The theme of this summit is his crucifixion in Jerusalem. Moses and Elijah who appeared to him in the clouds represent the prophetic tradition in Judaism. While Peter proposes to construct three tents to privatize this experience (an attitude that is found in contemporary market-oriented spirituality!), Jesus wants his disciples to go with him down to the valley of disfiguration where the disciples confront the stark human realities. What is lacking in the present youth is this synthesis in their spiritual outlook. What we need is an integral spiritual vision and mission. It is high time that we develop an awareness that prophetic spirituality is not to negate everything without a concrete involvement in the community to create new situations and systems. Similarly, mystic spirituality is not a flight into spiritual fantasies and self-righteousness and a 'holier than thou' attitude!

Jesus says, "Blessed are the peace makers…" The peace that he gives is not merely inner consolation or a superficial state of mind which is non-committal, but he commissions his followers to be involved in the mission of peace making. More than ever before, in the context of war, hatred, communal strife, family crisis, and so on, the world stands in dire need of this peace. This means that we can have inner peace only in and through our efforts to promote peace in the world.

9. Kingdom as the Reign of God

Life becomes authentic when we make it a vocation. A sense of vocation enables us to discern the sanctity and the 'beyond dimension' of life. Here we have to raise some of the ultimate questions such as "What is the meaning of my life?", "What is the purpose of my life?","What should I do in my life?", and so on. According to Paul Tillich, the famous theologian of the 20th century, "*That which concerns us ultimately is divine.*" Discernment of our vocation is human response to God's call in our lives. In other words, God would never impose His will on human beings. Rather, He inspires, motivates, guides, and leads. The challenge before us is always to opt for life, to choose life (Deut. 30:19), or to promote the symbols of life at all levels.

C. S. Song, one of the prominent Asian writers, prefers to use the term 'Reign of God' instead of the Kingdom as he considers 'Kingdom' terminology as product of the monarchic period. Song attempts to reflect on the person and work of Christ within the framework of the reign of God. He subtly makes this point in the following words:

> *The reign of God is the key. Jesus without it is a disincarnated person – a person without a body. Jesus separated from it is a theological construct that doesn't connect to reality. Jesus only loosely connected with it is a phantom that preoccupies the doctrinal interest of the religious authorities but haunts the hearts of the people in the streets. Jesus without the reign of God is an incomplete Jesus.*[5]

In other words, Jesus is the enabler, the facilitator, and the visible embodiment of the reign of God. Here God's reign means freedom and a passion for truth and justice. The question is not whether we should replace the term 'Kingdom of God' with the 'reign of God.' This has to do with the limitations of the language that we use in theology. What is of great importance is to note that the Kingdom of God or the reign of God is God's doing in the world with genuine human participation. As mentioned earlier, here we have to do away with all notions of Christian triumphalism and aggressiveness. What matters are the values of God's reign, such as freedom, love, equality, and justice.

10. Mission of the Kingdom

Mission is basically God's doing in the world. Human beings are co-workers with God in the establishment and furtherance of His mission. God's mission in the world begins with creation. The whole created order is the agenda of God's mission. Jesus Christ is God's ultimate missionary on earth. Christian mission should always be on Christ's way. Mission is both our being and doing. It is not to be seen as one of the activities of the church. The goal of mission is not the communal propaganda of the Church, but the proclamation and promotion of the Kingdom of God as taught and lived by Christ.

The word 'mission' is not found in the Bible; instead, the word 'witness 'is used. The task of the Church is to give witness to Christ and His Kingdom through concrete manifestations in history. A witness is always answerable, vulnerable, and accountable. What matters here is the credibility of our witness. Biblical scholars point out that the Greek word *marturia,* which is translated as 'witness' also denotes 'martyr.' This has to do with the costly and committed witness of the church, which involves definite stances with Christ in our personal and social life. This is how Emilio Castro summarizes the Mission mandate of the church:

> *In the perspective of the Kingdom the church is called to be and to go. To be an anticipation of the Kingdom; to show in its internal life the values of justice and supportive love; to develop a priestly servant vocation, in interceding in Abrahamic tradition, in anticipation, the coming of the Kingdom; to watch, like the virgins of the parable, for the coming of the Lord, and then to be the missionary people of God, called and sent all over the world to proclaim and serve, announcing and manifesting the coming of the Kingdom of God.*[6]

Mission is understood in a variety of ways in Christian traditions: as liberation, as humanization, as proclamation of the Kingdom of God, as development, as building up of the community, as dialogue, as healing the brokenness in the world, as Christian presence, and so on. While underscoring all these dimensions of mission, what is significant here is the element of hope that we nourish in and through our mission work. Here we have to remind ourselves that the purpose of mission is not to extend the boundaries of the Church but a meaningful Christian presence in the community. This is not to be a threatening presence to people of other faiths but a healing, reconciling, and transforming presence.

The following words of Martin Luther King Jr. prior to his assassination in Memphis, Tennessee on April 4, 1968 should reverberate in our Christian vocation:

> "*Human progress never rolls in on the wheels of inevitability; it comes through the tireless efforts of men and women willing to be co-workers with God and without this hard work time itself becomes an ally of the forces of social stagnation. We must use time creatively, in the knowledge that the time is always ripe to do right.*"

The Kingdom of God can be understood as a dynamic becoming; a movement with Christ till the fullness of eternity. This can be seen as an integral approach to mission.

Mission is God's continuing activity through the spirit to mend the brokenness of creation, to overcome the fragmentation of humanity, and to heal the rift between humanity, nature and God.[7] This is not the mission of the church to those outside. It is done along with those who are in search for the wholeness of life and those who share the burden of broken relationship between God and humans, humans among themselves, and humans and nature. The important question for us is not what God is doing with our churches but rather what God is doing through us and how can we discern where Christ is at work and respond to him. Raymond Fung in a striking article "*Evangelism today: Sinners and sinned-againstness*" underlines the need to emphasize the "sinned against"-ness in our mission. In the light of his own experiences in Hong Kong, he calls for a "*sharpening of our understanding of the people as 'sinned–against', not in a behaviouristic sense but in a theological sense.*"[8] The central thrust here is to take the dimension of sin seriously in all its deadly and oppressive forms in our mission.

A radical departure from the colonial, expansionistic, triumphant model of mission is evident in postcolonial reflections on mission. The new awareness that mission is not the geographical expansion of the church or a communal propaganda of Christianity as a religion but the willingness to be with God to heal the brokenness at different levels should be heard afresh in our mission praxis.

Very often, the element of universalism is considered as the one that is more conducive to the mission of the church than Jewish particularism and the so-called Christian exclusivism. The usual argument is that universalism has more space for other traditions, cultures and ideologies. For example, God's creation in its entirety is within the framework of universalism. This challenges the church to be sensitive to the issues such as human rights, gender justice, marginalization of the poor, etc. But the post colonialists would strike a different note here. As Paul Lakeland points out:

> "*Unfortunately, Christian universalism has produced the opposite effects. Rather than a basis for equality, Christianity more often has built hierarchies of domination and submission. In relation to non-Christians, universalism has been a rationale for conquest and persecution.*"[9]

Even the "Great Commission" mandate has been used over the decades as a divine justification for colonial expansion. For example, in India we have had British imperialism along with evangelization. Hence, a conscientious departure from the colonial-triumphalist-conquest model of mission is inevitable. The task should be to bridge the gap between the inherited traditions and new situations. What is desirable is the coming together of all like-minded, life-affirming, peace-loving people for the furtherance of God's mission in our times.

We need to honestly examine whether we truly manifest the Kingdom of God in our life and mission. Is the Kingdom our first priority or have we deviated from its vision because of our structural compulsions and institutional mundanities? Is the Kingdom of God only a topic of our preaching or do we have a real praxis on mission? Let us continuously remind ourselves that our church life and mission should be evaluated in the light of its proximity to or alienation from the Kingdom and its values. What we need is the discernment to see what God is doing in the world through the church and outside the church in the furtherance of the Kingdom and promotion of hope to all. Let us wind up this section with the following prayer:

> God, come to us and journey with us so that we may walk in your grace and peace.
>
> Fill us with hope so that we may break through barriers.
>
> Inspire us on our ecumenical journey, making possible encounters and dialogue.
>
> Send your Spirit to strengthen us in our prophetic role of proclaiming liberation.
>
> May your Spirit be a gentle breeze when we need comfort and security.
>
> But let it be a strong wind when we are too settled and need to speak out.
>
> Let your life-giving peace come into our bodies and be expressed in action for peace between people, between churches, religions and between nations.
>
> May your transforming grace inspire us to join hands and declare the freedom given by your love.
>
> Shower your blessings upon us as we journey on, announcing the good news of justice, caring and acceptance.[10]

7

The Day of the Lord and the Son of Man

The first part of this chapter has to do with the Old Testament concept of the Day of the Lord. The attempt here is to see to how the concept was developed in the history of Judaism; how did the prophets re-interpret the concept and also how it is used in the New Testament narratives. The second part has to do with a realistic expectation of the Last Day; especially in the context of some of the heresies and cults in Christian faith. The third part examines the concept of the Son of Man, a title that Jesus preferred to use for himself. The focus is that the prophetic corrective to the Jewish understanding of the Day of the Lord should be given due attention, especially in our effort to articulate the person and work of Jesus.

The concept of the *Day of the Lord* and *Son of Man* have their roots in the Jewish tradition. The Jews always looked forward to the day of the Lord in their time of distress and historical ambiguities such as war, natural catastrophes, etc. The prophets have tried to give a new dimension to the concept of the Day of the Lord and the Son of Man, which was not easy for the people to digest.

1. Day of the Lord

The doctrine of the Day of the Lord is found mainly in the Old Testament, especially in the Prophetic books. This is a special expression which designates God's solemn interventions in the course of history. Sometimes it is presented as 'the Day' or 'that Day.' It has a two-fold meaning: First, it is a historical event, the Day which will witness the triumph of God over his enemies. And second, it has a cultic meaning, the Day that is especially set aside for the worship of God.[1]

In the Old Testament, this theme is presented as the decisive intervention of God in the life of Israel. The Jewish apocalyptic eschatology regarded the time in two stages: The *present age* which was altogether bad and evil, incapable of being cured and fit only for destruction. Then there was *the age to come,* which was the golden age of God and of Jewish supremacy. But in between the two, there would be *the Day of the Lord,* which would be the terrible time of cosmic upheaval and destruction, the desperate birth-pangs of the new age.[2]

In the prophetic books, it is referred to as the 'Day of light', the Day of Yahweh (Eze. 30:3; Isa. 13:6), and as a day of clouds and fire. The destruction of Jerusalem was considered as the 'Day of Yahweh' (Eze. 13:5, Isa. 9:3). In the liturgical life of the church, the Day of the Lord is referred to as Sunday. This day doesn't replace the Jewish Sabbath, as it is popularly understood. But rather, it commemorates a historical event that is so decisive in the life of the church; the glorious resurrection of the Lord over the powers of death. In each Eucharistic celebration on Sunday, the church proclaims the return of the Lord, his *parousia* (1 Cor. 11:26). In the liturgy of the Mar Thoma Church, we say, "Your death, O Lord, we commemorate; your resurrection we celebrate; and your Second Coming we await." In 2 Thessalonians, Paul makes it clear that 'the Day of the Lord' is not the collapse of the space-time universe – "*Please don't be suddenly blown off in your thinking, or be unsettled, either through spiritual influence, or through a word, or through a letter supposedly from us, telling you that the day of the Lord has already arrived*" (2 Thess. 2:2).

2. Expectation of the Last Day

As mentioned earlier, the emphasis is that Yahweh is the one who directs history to its culmination. "*Yahweh directs history to its final outcome. Hence, the proclamation for Israel of a Day of Yahweh will become a proclamation of such a Day for the whole world. This day will not occur in the course of time, but at the end of time of our present world.*"[3] The prophets tried to reinterpret the 'Day of the Lord', mainly because of the false hope in the community of Israel. For example, they believed that they had some kind of divine immunity; that they would be delivered from all their troubles, and their enemies unconditionally. So the prophets brought to the fore the concept of a remnant which shows God's redemptive love in spite of their historical alienation from his ways and disobedience to the covenant. Contrary to the popular belief about the Day of the Lord, as a day of light, victory and so on, Amos strikes a different note:

> *"How terrible it will be for you who long for the day of the Lord! What good will that day do to you? For you it will be a day of darkness and not of light. It will be like a man who runs from a lion and meets a bear! Or like a man who comes home and rested his hand on the wall only to be bitten by a snake! The day of the Lord will bring darkness and not light; it will be a day of gloom, without any brightness"* (Amos 5:18-20).

Then Amos talks about the expectations of the Lord in unequivocal words: "*Let justice flow like a stream and righteousness like a river that never goes dry.*"(vs. 24)Amos' version of the day of the Lord is a rediscovery of the concept. As a social critique, the prophet challenges all false notions of the day of the Lord which led to his conflict with the priesthood. The prophet highlights the covenant obligations and the Law which are justice and righteousness.

In Ezekiel, the Day of the Lord is given as the end of time (Ez 7:6).In Daniel it is the end of the world (Dan 9:26). In the New Testament, the Day of the Lord is presented as the Day of the Lord Jesus (1 Thes 5:2; 2 Thes 2:2).

According to New Testament scholars, in the Greco-Roman world, *parousia* was used to denote the official visitation of the Roman emperors. The early church had the concept of an imminent *parousia.* This was in the light of their Easter and Pentecost experiences. This led to several doctrinal deviations and also unwillingness to work among the believers. Paul addresses this issue in 2 Thessalonians. Instead of saying that the *parousia* would be at the end, Paul exhorts them to be vigilant in their journey of faith. Paul also says, "*While we still have time, let us do good*"(Col 4:5; Eph 5:16).

Peter admonishes the early believers who had difficulty in the delay of the *parousia.* According to him, it is because The Lord doesn't measure time as human beings. "*But do not ignore this one fact, beloved, that with the Lord one day is like a thousand years, and a thousand years are like one day.*"(2 Pet 3:8) Another insight that Peter gives is more significant: the Lord's coming is delayed because he looks forward to the conversion of all. In other words, the Lord doesn't want anyone to be perished for ever. But contrary to this Biblical vision, very often, the end time enthusiasts declare the inevitability of hell or eternal condemnation of the sinners!

3. The Son of Man

The title, Son of Man, has its origin in the Old Testament and Judaism. The expression 'son of man' occurs frequently in the Old Testament as a synonym for 'man.' Most of the references are on human finitude, one's smallness before God and so on: "*You tell man to return to what he was; you change him back to dust.*" (Ps 90:3) Sometimes it refers to human sinful condition: "*The Lord looks down from heaven at mankind to see if there are any who are wise, and who worship him.*" (Ps 14:2) The Palmist is wonder stuck as to such a feeble person is crowned by God as the crown of creation: "*Who is man that you are mindful of him; the son of man that you care for him?*"(Ps 8:5) Before God human beings are nothing; yet God is counting on them.

In Daniel, we have the vision of the eschatological Son of Man who exercises authority over the beast; the Babylonian Empire, according to Old Testament scholars.

> *I saw in the night visions; behold, one like'the son of Man' came with the clouds of heaven, and came to the ancient of days, and they brought him near before him. And he was given dominion, and glory, and a kingdom that all peoples, nations and languages, should serve him: his dominion is*

an everlasting dominion, which shall not pass away, and his kingdom that which shall not be destroyed (Dan 7:13-14).

This is a new perspective on the term 'son of man' from that used in the Psalms. Some suggest here an Iranian myth of a primordial man returning as saviour at the end of time.[4] The Jewish apocalyptic after the Book of Daniel took over this idea of the 'son of man' and interpreted as a mysterious being with God, possessing justice and revealing God's salvific deeds for the end time. The New Testament usage of the 'son of Man' is a continuation of this Old Testament tradition.

In the Gospels, the usage *son of man* is found seventy times. The *son of man* is the New Testament title that Jesus always preferred to use for himself. This title is used in three different ways.

One: Man in an ordinary way. For example, when a scribe wanted to follow Jesus, Jesus says, "*Foxes have holes and birds of the air have nests, but the son of man has nowhere to lay his head*" (Mt 8:20).

Two: Jesus' present sufferings and imminent death. "*And he began to teach them that the son of man must suffer many things, and be rejected by the elders and the chief priests and the scribes, and be killed after three days he will rise again.*" (Mk 8:31).

"*For the son of man came not to be served but to serve and to give his life as a ransom for many*" (Mk 10:45).

Three: The eschatological son of man. "*Soon after the trouble of those days, the sun will grow dark and the moon will no longer shine, the stars will fall from heaven, and the powers from space will be driven from their courses. Then the sign of the Son of Man will appear in the sky; and all the peoples of the earth will weep as they see that the Son of Man coming on the clouds of heaven with power and great glory. The great trumpet will sound, and he will send out his angels to the four corners of the earth, and they will gather his chosen people from one end of the world to the other*" (Mt 24:29-31).

The question that is very often asked is why did Jesus prefer this title: Is it because of its emphasis in Psalms regarding the finitude of human beings or is it because of the eschatological connotations? From the life and ministry of Jesus, it can be pointed out that Jesus never wanted to project himself as a super man or a miracle performer; he would rather identify himself with the suffering servant in Isaiah.

We have a similar text by Paul in 1Thessalonians,[4] on the eschatological Son of Man.

What we are teaching you now is the Lord's teaching: we who are alive on the Day when the Lord comes will not go ahead of those who have died. There will be the shout of command, the archangel's voice, the sound of God's trumpet, and the Lord himself will come down from heaven. Those who have died believing in Christ will rise to life first; then we who are living at that time will be gathered up along with them in the clouds to meet the Lord. So then, encourage one another with these words (1 Thes 4:13-18).

These words are very often read in our burial services as the sure words of consolation to the bereaved. Among the texts given above, though they are all interrelated, the texts' pointing to the eschatological 'Son of Man' needs more exploration. A few concerns here are the following:

One: Do we need to underscore a worldview which gives a three-layered world? For example, heaven above, earth below and the Hades underneath.

Two: Is angelology an essential part of Christian faith?

Three: Did Jesus and Paul look forward to an imminent end of the world?

Four: How do we explain these apocalyptic imageries, especially the arrival of the Son of Man in the clouds?

Five: Is there a Gnostic redeemer myth here? In the Gnostic redeemer myth, a heavenly being is sent down from the world of light to the earth, which has fallen under the sway of demonic powers, in order to liberate the sparks of light, which have their origin in the world of light, but owing to a fall in primeval times, have been compelled to inhabit human bodies. This emissary takes a human form and carries out the work entrusted to him by the Father, as a result he is not cut off from the Father. He reveals himself in his utterances, and so reveals himself... and also teaches them the way to return to their home, to which he as a redeemed Redeemer, rises again.[5]

Six: Is there a conflict with the prophetic eschatology which emphasizes 'continuity' with the earth and an apocalyptic eschatology, as mentioned here which emphasizes 'discontinuity'? Some of the issues here are the following:

- Is the concept of the Day of the Lord a privatized, ahistorical one?
- Does this concept enable us to take our life of discipleship seriously?
- Is it an inclusive concept or an exclusive one: As if the Lord comes to rescue the Christians and condemns others?
- What do we expect the Lord to usher in? A system of justice and righteousness for all?
- Can we wait for the Lord doing His will along with all people of 'good will'?

The message of the Day of the Lord and Son of Man is clear: God is in control of history. When we look forward to his intervention, we must have a clear vision of God's wider family on earth. We cannot privatize God since God has his own ways of doing things in the world. The prophetic critique of the concept of the Day of the Lord should reverberate within us in our journey of faith.

Our concern should be a God centered community where justice and righteousness will flourish. In order to accomplish this task, as pointed out earlier, we need to discern the signs of the times; the efforts that are under way and the people who are committed to promoting these values. An introspection of the life and mission of the Church becomes essential here. To what extent do we promote justice within our systems and structures?

Emilio Castro, the former General Secretary of W.C.C, was one of the main speakers at the Maramon Convention, in Kerala, several years ago. In his brief introduction, after acknowledging the presence of an ancient Christian community in Kerala, he raised a few concerns:

- What does it mean to be a Christian community?
- Does it mean that you have a system that is just and righteous?
- Does it mean than human life has more value and worth here?
- Does it mean that your presence as a community is a healing and reconciling presence?
- Does it mean that human rights and freedom are promoted at any cost?
- Does it mean that you have an effective parenting programme with in the Church?

Well, it should be acknowledged that a few of these concerns are being addressed at the different levels of the church. Nevertheless, there are several areas which are deficient in the manifestations of the above concerns.

8

The Cross and Resurrection of Jesus Christ

The concern of this chapter is a re-examination of the cross and resurrection of Jesus Christ as the central events in Christian eschatological discourse. In the first part, a few approaches to the cross are evaluated with the focus on the meaning of the "faith appropriation of the cross." The concern is to say that the "faith appropriation of the cross" should lead us to "a genuine life of commitment on the way of the cross." The second part is the theological significance of the cross; the emphasis here is the participation in the passion of Christ through concrete historical actions. The third part deals with the ethical dimensions of the cross and resurrection of Jesus. The emphasis here is that resurrection is always on the way of the cross; for Jesus and for all those who follow him. What matters here is a "costly obedience to God" (Bonhoeffer).

The cross and resurrection of Jesus Christ are two deeply related events in Christian eschatology. What is required of us in this context is a 'seeing in depth' of these events rather than searching for factual details or objective verifications. Unless the resurrected Jesus is confessed as the crucified Lord, the resurrection will become the ground for Christian triumphalism and a facile affirmation of the world. A question can be asked as to why the Jewish authorities wanted to crucify Jesus which is a Roman capital punishment? It's true that most of the charges leveled against Jesus were of the 'blasphemy type' such as the breaking of Sabbath laws etc. A few reflections are given below:

One: Roman Government was in power and the religious laws are within the framework of the State laws. This is the situation even in the 21st century democratic societies.

Two: The followers of Jesus were mostly from the Roman, Gentile background; and only a few came from the Jewish background. Hence, the Jewish authorities wanted to extinguish both Jesus and his movement in its entirety; both within Judaism and Roman societies.

Three: Crucifixion was a common capital punishment in those days and it was so cruel, barbaric and demonic. Such a punishment would be a lesson and warning to the would-be followers of Jesus everywhere.

1. What Does the Cross Mean? Different Approaches to the Cross

In Jesus' days, the cross was a capital punishment in Rome; mainly for the political prisoners –those who challenge Roman Imperialism and also for the slaves who run away from their masters. Then, why is it said that two thieves were also crucified with Jesus on either side? It has been pointed out by New Testament scholars that they were not just thieves who were booked for theft, but political prisoners, perhaps who were caught for guerrilla warfare against Roman regime. Roman history points out that hundreds of political prisoners were crucified prior to Jesus. The Biblical narratives say that two forces were behind the crucifixion of Jesus: Roman Government and Judaism. In contemporary language, the unholy nexus between the state and religion! But the Jewish hierarchy wanted to create a political charge against Jesus. The question of paying taxes is one such trap!

The following approaches to the cross can be found in the church and outside:

a. Secular Approach

Mahatma Gandhi, Martin Luther King Jr., and several others in history have used the cross as a symbolic weapon in their fight for justice and freedom. In literature also, the cross and resurrection are used as powerful symbols. There are non-Christian poets in Malayalam, like O. N. V. Kurup, Aiyyappa Panikker, and others, who have used these symbols effectively in their poems.

b. Ritualization of the Cross

Here cross is considered almost as a cultic object of worship and prayers are offered before the cross for special favours! Rather than the cross, the crucifix is considered as the cultic object of worship in the Roman Catholic tradition. Cross is also used here as an object of veneration and worship. In the Eastern Tradition, there is no crucifix, as more significance is given to the risen Christ. As Dr Sebastian Kappen an Indian Jesuit thinker rightly reminds us, "*The ritualization of the Cross is a deliberate attempt to do away with the cause of Christ.*"

c. Idolization of the Cross

Some of the dominant images during the Middle Ages were the 'Bleeding face of Christ', 'the Sacred blood of Christ', 'the Sacred heart of Christ', and so on. Though the cross is an important symbol in Christian faith, any attempt to make a cult of the cross or to attribute magical powers to it are to be questioned.

In Kerala, recently another image of the cross caught media attention. In the protected Western Ghats of the State, a group of Christians planted a few crosses and started occupation of the land! The government had to act swiftly and the so-called 'invading crosses' had to be removed!

d. Prediction-fulfilment

The approach here is that all deeds of Jesus were predicted earlier by the prophets and when he did some things; he was simply fulfilling those perdictions. The issue here is that the definite choice of Jesus, his self-will and obedience to the Father, are totally ignored.

e. Faith Appropriation of the Cross

This is a typical Christian approach. The belief that "Jesus died for my sins; and when I accept him as my saviour who died for my sins on the cross, I am saved." While accepting the devotional value of life; the issue here is that the inevitability of the cross in the life of Jesus vis-à-vis our life, is ignored here.

f. Participation in the Passion of Jesus

The challenge of Jesus is this: If anyone would like to follow me, let him/her deny himself/herself, take up their cross and follow me (Mk. 8:34). Paul also highlights this dimension: "*Those have been baptized into Christ have been baptized into his death…*" (Rom 6:3).

2. Theological Significance of the Cross

Now let us try to understand the meaning of the cross.

a. Divine Necessity and Choice of Jesus

The cross was a divine necessity as well as the choice of Jesus. Cross is not simply the wooden piece on which Jesus was nailed to death. Rather, it is the consequence of Jesus' mission, his bold stances against the forces of sin and evil. The Biblical records say that even after knowing that he would be crucified and few of his disciples were going to be the allies of the Roman Government to extinguish him, he loved them all till the end!

b. Salvation is on the Way of the Cross

In other words, our salvation is not on the object of the cross; but on the way – in our obedience to Christ for the fulfilment of the value of the Kingdom of God. Here we are not simply at the receiving end of salvation; rather we are called to be with Christ in His salvific mission in the world.

c. The Pain Love of God

On the cross of Christ, we see that God participates in human suffering. This is the *kenotic* (self-giving) dimension of the cross. This is a reversal of the God concept in the Greco-Roman world where god was beyond sufferings. The pain dimension of Christian faith is a new contribution. Kazav Kitamoris' article on "*The Theology of the Pain of God*" brings it out so powerfully:

> "*His will for salvation is manifested in the person of Jesus Christ as his pain. The glory of the cross reflects the radiance of his face...the pain of God gives meaning and value to human suffering.*"[1]

In other words, what Jesus offers to his followers is not safety and security here and a safe place in heaven; but rather a costly commitment with him.

d. God's Solidarity with all Those who Stand for Truth and Justice in History

A question that is very often asked is what is the meaning of martyrdom, or those whose lives are at risk due to their particular choices for justice and truth. This is the paradigmatic significance of the Cross which continuously reminds us that our efforts for the transformation of unjust systems are not in vain. The suffering, rejection, and persecution are not lost forever and there is value in our stance for Christ and his Kingdom.

> In Jesus' admonition to the scribes and Pharisees, he says, "*Therefore I send you prophets, wise men and scribes, some of whom you will kill and crucify; and some you will flog in your synagogues, and persecute from town to town, so that on you may come all the righteous blood shed on earth, from the blood of righteous Abel, to the blood of Zechariah, son of Barachiah.*" (Mt 23:34-35) Here, we have the paradigmatic significance of the cross. The blood that is shed for righteous causes in history has its own redeeming value.

e. Obedience to God on the Way of the Cross Makes our Life Significant

As pointed out earlier, here cross is not a distant object to be venerated but a way of life which is inevitably the "crucified mind" over against a "crusading mind", as Kosuke Koyama points out.

f. Resurrection is Always on the Way of the Cross

In other words, the cross and resurrection are heavily interwoven. The annual regularity of Lent can dilute its seriousness and make it ritualistic and casual. Let us be reminded of the fact that this period is set apart to usher in certain new values in our life of faith; values that are conducive to the furtherance of the Kingdom of God and its righteousness. Lent also reminds us of an important paradox in our faith that the way of life is through suffering and death. This was our Lord's response to the Greeks: "*I am telling you the truth; a grain of wheat remains no more than a single grain unless it is dropped into the ground and dies. If it does die, then it produces many grains.*" (Jn.12:24) The power of evil in history is real. We should not underestimate the socio-political and religious structures of evil. When we say that the power of the cross overcomes evil; it is not some kind of a tit for tat or a magical power of the cross; but the suffering love of God. "*Because of the cross we cannot live in facile optimism about history. The cross signifies God's recognition of the power of evil. It also shows how God deals with evil. Jesus' encounter with evil leads to the cross, and to the vindication of love in the resurrection.*"[2]

Here is an unequivocal affirmation that the way of life is not the way of domination, power, or subjugation but inevitably the way of the Cross.

3. Ethical Significance of the Cross

a. Cross as the Pattern of Reconciliation

The symbol of the cross reminds us of God's reconciling work in the world. In Ephesians 2:16 and Colossians 1:10, the reconciling power of the cross is brought to the fore. The pattern of the cross has been emphasized by many in the Christian church and outside. It is only in our clear stances with Christ and for Christ in the ministry of reconciliation that we become the real followers of Christ on the way of the cross. In other words, rather than any cultic observance of the Passion of Christ, our preparedness to be broken with Christ for the ministry of reconciliation is what makes our faith significant.

> "*Jesus is the suffering Messiah, but he suffers in order to end suffering. Only through this suffering can the mission of Jesus Christ be understood.*"[3] In other words, we should not romanticize suffering as it was done in the Middle ages in Europe. Nevertheless, the cross of Christ serves as a paradigm in our life of faith which constantly tells us that the stances for justice and truth are painful but not in vain.

Jesus Christ challenges us with new questions in our areas of professional excellence. He wants us to be his agents of reconciliation within the church and outside the church. The resurrection of Christ points out that the forces of sin and evil do not have the final word in history. Nevertheless, in the process of reconciliation, the forces of sin that are embedded in today's socio-political systems are not to be condoned. The report of the Commission on Truth and Reconciliation in South Africa is a case in point here. The Commission was appointed immediately after the sweeping victory of the African National Congress. Rather than promoting any polemical attitudes and triumphalism, the Commission underscored the necessity of reconciliation to heal the wounds created by the Apartheid regime. These words are to be heard afresh in our contemporary situations of violence and conflict.

Christian discipleship is always on the way of the Cross. Jesus chose his twelve disciples to be with him, to caste out demons and to preach the good news of the Kingdom (Mk. 3:15). In other words, Jesus wanted them to be with him on the way of the cross. Nevertheless, a careful reading of the Passion narratives in the Gospels will reveal that all his disciples miserably failed to be with him till his final agony and crucifixion. Hence, even at the point of the culmination of his earthly ministry, Jesus had to alert them to 'stay awake.'

b. What is Resurrection Faith?

The concept of resurrection is considered as one of the basic tenets of Christian faith. Even though the truth of resurrection is central to the Gospel narratives, the 'how' of resurrection is not the concern of the Bible. In other words, the Bible does not talk about the mechanics of the resurrection of Jesus Christ.

This is not simply an affirmation of a historical fact, that on the third day after the crucifixion Jesus rose from the dead. This is also not to be made as the basis for Christian triumphalism and exclusivism. Faith in resurrection means that death is not the end of life and God will not allow sin and evil to say the final word in history. In other words, resurrection is the triumph of life in every way. Hence, faith in resurrection enables us to overcome all tendencies of fatalism and determinism. In the Indian context both these tendencies loom large; fatalism in Hindu spiritual circles and determinism in Christian spiritual circles. Both these tendencies are not helpful in the forward march of humanity towards fullness of life.

> As Jose Cardenas Pallares writes, "*Jesus is not a corpse; he is not the prisoner of death...God's future becomes present in this poor, destitute, disfigured, annihilated probate. This human being who was made into society's refuse has within him the life of God. The power of injustice and ambition, deceit, destruction, oppression, and money are rendered impotent before the life of God, the life that takes sides with the poor and the just.*"[4]

In the words of St. Paul, "*When we were baptized into union with Christ Jesus, we were baptized into union with his death. By our baptism, then, we were buried with him and shared his death in order that, just as Christ was raised from death by the glorious power of the Father, so also we might live a new life*" (Rom 6:3-5). In other words, a simplistic faith appropriation of the cross is not enough; what matters is our participation in the saving event of Christ. This is what we are asked to celebrate in our Eucharist. Rather than a superficial and cultic observance of the cross, our preparedness to be broken with Christ for the furtherance of the Kingdom of God is what makes our faith significant.

Bishop Tutu reminds us that "*The resurrection of Jesus Christ is not the revivification of a corpse. It is speaking about a tremendous reality; that Jesus is risen, his life is real, he is accessible to me...*"[5]

The resurrection of Christ constantly reminds us of the truth that evil has only temporal victory in this world and that death is not the end of life. This is also God's victory over the forces of sin and evil in the world. We can proclaim Jesus as the life of the world only through our life on the way of the cross and also by opting for life at all levels. What is required of us is a continuous assimilation of the mystery of the cross and resurrection in our times. This will definitely give new challenges, priorities, and values before us.

Hence, in our understanding of the cross and resurrection two temptations are to be specially avoided: a narrow, privatized, cultic representation of the cross and an attitude of triumphalism. In other words, what matters is not just an intellectual comprehension, acceptance, or rejection of the historicity of resurrection or a value-free approach to the event of resurrection. We have to allow ourselves to be continuously challenged by what Jesus did and taught; what is known as the 'Christ-event', i.e., the person and work of Christ. It also points to the fact that the way of life is through death. For example, the risen Jesus shows Thomas the scars in his body: "*Then he said to Thomas, put your finger here, and look at my hands; then stretch out your hand and put it in my side. Stop your doubting and believe*" (Jn. 20:27).

Along with the early Church, let us also say that He is risen indeed.

c. God of Life and the Idols of Death

As mentioned earlier, idols of death such as the idolatry of power, idolatry of wealth, idolatry of caste etc are found in all communities. In any attempt to transform the local spaces, these idolatrous elements are to be confronted with the power of the risen Christ. Our task here is to manifest Jesus Christ as the Lord of life over and against all powers of death at all levels. This is possible only through our partnership with all those who are allies of the higher values of life. Resurrection is the triumph of life which is beyond physical existence.

The theme of the 10th Assembly of the WCC in 2013 at Bursan, South Korea was "God of Life– Lead Us to Justice and Peace." Most of the WCC themes were Christocentric in nature in the latter half of 20th century. For example, for the New Delhi Assembly it was "Jesus Christ – the Light of the World" and for Nairobi Assembly it was "Jesus Christ Frees and Unites" and so on. Nevertheless, in the third millennium, there is shift in the selection of themes from Christocentric to Theocentric emphasis. For example, at Porto Alegre in 2005 it was "God in Your Grace Transform the World." This theme is a continuation of the reflections at Porto Alegre. According to many in the ecumenical field; this shift is to make the member churches more inclusive and relational in nature.

Here it should be remembered that we are not trying to suggest to God something that He has never thought of. We cannot give a mandate to God. Rather, at the heights of human self-sufficiency and autonomy of human reason – which is a product of enlightenment, science, technology, communication revolution, etc. – on the one hand and our contemporary historical predicaments, hate campaigns, violence, uncertainties, and 'walls of partition' on the other, we are trying to see afresh God's need in the transformation of the world. In other words, this theme is on the one hand a negation of all deterministic notions such political determinism, economic determinism, cultural determinism, etc. and on the other an affirmation of God's sovereignty over the created order. It is as if we are praying thus:

> *God, we acknowledge that this is your world, the entire creation belongs to you. We cannot transform this world without you. Sinners and sinned against as we are, we are sorry that we have tried to manage the affairs of this world without you. We thought we are unlimited and that we are on our own... Today, more than ever, we need you; we need your transforming presence, healing presence and reconciling presence in the world. Enable us to go with you into the world with your eyes, with your arms, with your Spirit. Amen.*[6]

What we have in the theme is a cry for life; a cry of the post-modern humanity who are at the zenith of human capabilities and potentials. According to Bishop William Temple, "*The proper outline of a Christian prayer is not please do for me what I want; but Lord, do in me, with me, and through me what you want.*" Prayer is also a rediscovery of God's presence in God's world and in our lives. Nevertheless, prayer is not an end in itself. So what we need in our times is acted prayers and prayerful actions. The genuineness of prayer is not the number of times or the amount of time we prayed but what kind of people we would become through our prayer. It would be nice if we can ponder on this question: Do we try to transform God, our situations, or ourselves through our prayers?

d. Costly Obedience as a Manifestation of Hope

The passion narratives are considered to be the first written documents in the New Testament. The other ones, such as miracle narratives, birth narratives, etc. were added on to them at a later stage. All these point to the relevance of the Christ event. The Johannine version of the Lord's Supper mentioned in John 13 is unique. In the Eastern tradition, the St. James liturgy is based on this narrative. Here the narrative is not the Last Supper, but an ordinary meal of Jesus along with the disciples towards the end of his ministry. Dr. Allen Walker, in one his messages at the Maramon Convention some years ago, drove home two sacraments that we need to underscore in the ministry of the Church: Bread and Wine, Towel and Basin! Both these are interrelated. Though we have many social welfare projects in the church, very often we don't see this inner connection between the two.

i. Re-enactment of the Passion of Christ

At the point of Jesus' impending death, rather than a ritual to be observed in memory of him, he was trying to interpret the meaning of his ultimate obedience to God. Later the church found sacramental value in this narrative. In Christian tradition over the decades, two responses to the passion can be discerned. Notwithstanding the significance of the first in our journey of faith, it is to be remembered that the obedience dimension of Christian faith is mainly in the participation in the passion of Christ. (Rom. 6:3ff) Rather than a dichotomy between the mystic and prophetic, what we need to underscore is a synthesis of both in the life and ministry of Christ, especially in his passion and death on the cross.

The question of Christology comes to the fore here. Very often a distinction is made between the classical and contemporary Christologies: the classical is obsessed with the question "Who is Jesus Christ" and the contemporary is more concerned with the question "Where is Jesus Christ"?

ii. Christ's Pattern of Obedience

As mentioned earlier, this is very often construed as 'prediction fulfilment.' Again, while underscoring a divine necessity of the way of the cross within the redemptive plan of God, let us not belittle the ultimate obedience of Christ unto the cross. In other words, the cross is to be seen as the consequence of the ultimate obedience of Christ in his march towards the Kingdom of God. As pointed out earlier he gives a similar call to those who would follow him (Mk. 8:34). Whom to obey becomes a pivotal question here (Acts. 4:19) In a powerful letter written to the South African Minister of Justice, in the context of the Apartheid regime, Allan Bosak, the South African theologian wrote: "*For a Christian, obedience to the state or any authority is always linked to the obedience to God. That is to say, obedience to human institutions is always relative...The believer in Christ has not only the right, but also the responsibility to be more obedient to God and God's law than to the Government, should the Government deviate from God's law.*"[7]

iii. Volitional Obedience

This is conscious and conscientious obedience. According to New Testament scholars, the Greek word *huppotaso* is used in Romans 13:1ff and Philippians 5:22ff.The question that comes to the fore is this: When Paul says, "*Be subject to the authority*", do we need to take it as an eternal doctrine about the state? What if the state goes wrong and demonic? Similarly, in family life, if the husband doesn't keep any family values, what is expected of the wife is not blind obedience to him but 'conscious obedience.' What we need to cherish in our church is also this dimension of obedience.

iv. Costly Obedience

This is a unique contribution of Dietrich Bonhoeffer, the German Theologian and leader of the Confessing Church, who had to pay a heavy price for his ultimate obedience to God during the Nazi regime in Germany. Resistance to undemocratic and authoritarian power systems becomes inevitable in a genuine Christian obedience. What we need to cherish in the church is a general framework of discipline and obedience. Here the church ought to become a spiritual home for all; in other words, a family of bishops, clergy and laity.

In the Orthodox and Mar Thoma traditions, when a person is consecrated as an episcopa, the congregation would say "*oxios.*" There is a wrong notion among the consecrated and the people at large, as if *oxios* means qualified or spiritually fit to *rule* over others in God's name! But according to the early church tradition there were occasions when a person was identified as a candidate for episcopal consecration, and the candidate flees and the people would forcibly bring him back and say '*oxios*' which really meant "You are qualified to be a *martyr* for us"! Well, what are the qualifications that we expect from our Bishops and clergy today? Here it is to be remembered that leadership, especially episcopacy was a dangerous enterprise in the early church; it was definitely a costly obedience to the Lord.

In an ordination sermon titled as '*Watchman and Shepherds*', Dr. S. J. Samartha highlights the task of the watchman (Eze. 33:1-9) and the responsibility of the shepherd (Jn. 10:16). According to him, "*The question for us is not whether to be watchmen or shepherds, but when to be watchmen and when to be shepherds to our people. The sense of discernment required here depends very much on the scriptural depth, theological strength and pastoral sensitivity of the shepherd.*"[8]

Though there is always a gap between the ideal and actual in human life, in a genuine attempt to revitalize the ministry of the church, a re-discovery of the essential nature of our pastoral ministry is inevitable. But the question we have to ponder on, due to our structural compulsions, systemic predicaments or church polity, is whether the non-essential functions loom large and the core functions have eroded. The context in which we are called to obey God as historical human beings is becoming more and more complex. Oversimplified answers to the complex issues of human life are counterproductive. What we need in our times is a new culture of obedience to God within our ecclesial traditions. As M. M. Thomas rightly reminds us "*Our task is to make the message of Jesus Christ intelligible in this generation and a choice for or against him inescapable.*"

Lastly, what is the hope element in the Cross and Resurrection of Christ? As pointed out earlier, the cross doesn't remove our pain but gives a new dimension to it. Let me try to slightly deviate from the traditional Christian understanding. Very often we say that salvation is on the Cross and the dimension of hope is in the resurrection. But, my submission is this: Rather than ritualizing and romanticizing the event of the cross; we need to internalize the pain-love (agape) of the cross and manifest it in our words and deeds. Here we are participating in the hope that God gives to all those who are suffering and neglected through our solidarity with them. Those who are affected by COVID-19, their families who are vulnerable, the health workers across the world who are doing a commendable and risky job are all in dire need of this hope; the hope that God has not given up on us; and His empowering presence is with us. In other words, our hope is a shared hope; we cannot privatize it.

9

Ascension and the Return of Jesus Christ

We have the doctrine of ascension and the return of Jesus only in the Synoptic Gospels and Book of Acts. In the Gospel of John, after the resurrection, Jesus gives the Holy Spirit to the disciples. "*Jesus said to them again, peace be with you. And when he had said this, he breathed on them and said to them, 'Receive the Holy Spirit.'*" (Jn. 20:21-22) This action of Jesus resonates with the creation account in Genesis: "*Then the Lord formed the man out of dust from the ground and breathed into his nostrils the breath of life, and the man became a living creature.*" (Gen. 2:7-8) In Genesis it is creation and in John it is new creation. Both are the actions of the Holy Spirit. Rather than the absence of the ascension and the return in John, let us ponder on the emphasis of this doctrine in the Synoptic Gospels.

1. The Doctrine of Ascension

The ascension and return of Christ are deeply interwoven. While Jesus was a historical human being he was within the limitations of time and space. For example, he didn't travel all over the world. He didn't speak all languages. His message of the Kingdom was made known only in a limited area of the world. In other words, he had linguistic, cultural, and geographical limitations. How can this Jesus be acknowledged as the Lord of the universe? The answer to this question is found in the doctrine of the ascension of Christ.

Hence, the ascension of Christ is not to be seen as an 'absentee Lordship'; in other words, the ascension means that Christ transcends all historical limitations (linguistic, cultural, geographical etc.) so that he could be with us all the time. Yes, the ascension then means the eternal availability of Christ.

Through his glorious ascension on the 40th day after the resurrection, he transcends all the limitations so that he can be with us always. In other words, rather than an escape into another world, or a flight to the outer space to return on another occasion; the ascension means the eternal availability of God in Jesus Christ.

As Bishop Deshmond Tutu writes so tellingly:

"*When we say Jesus ascended into heaven, you don't believe that he got into a kind of ecclesiastical life that took him into the stratosphere. This is the language that is being used figuratively because the realities that are being described are not human realities; they are supra-natural realities.*"[2]

Jesus' saying after the Great Commission of the disciples sounds relevant here: "*I am with you till the end of the age*" (Mt. 28:20b).

We can derive certain insights from this event:

- Jesus Christ is not the private property of Christianity or the church. As Raymond Panikker points out: If Christ is the Lord of the universe; then every point in the universe has a claim on Christ.
- The mission of Christ is a continuum; He is with us in a new way so that His mission would be continued on earth.
- As it was announced at the time of his birth, "Glory to God in the highest of heavens and peace on earth among those with whom he is pleased" (Lk. 2:14); the ascended Christ is among all people of good will.
- Ascension also challenges us to transcend all our narrow loyalties; linguistic, cultural, ethnic and clannish barriers and to be more open to all others, who are all allies of the higher values of life.

The event of Pentecost and the Pentecost lifestyle of the early church are mentioned in Acts. 2. We have here the nucleus of the church – the new community in the power of the Spirit. The miracle of Pentecost is the miracle of communication. Though the Holy Spirit has been present in the world ever since the creation of the world, the church receives the Spirit in a special way on the day of Pentecost to inculcate the values of the Kingdom of God as taught and lived by Jesus Christ. The Spirit gives us conviction about sin, righteousness, and judgment (Jn 16:8).

Metaphors such as 'water', 'fire', 'wind', 'dove', and 'oil' are used in the Bible to describe the Spirit. These refer to the different operative dimensions of the Holy Spirit. The gifts of the Spirit are given to the believers for the edification of the community of faith (1 Cor. 12:7). It is our task to rekindle the work of the Spirit within us through fervent prayer, meditation, and participation in the saving deeds of God in the world. Let us constantly remind ourselves that the Holy Spirit gives us the divine energy for an authentic life in the world. Rather than making exclusive truth claims about the power and gifts of the Spirit, the challenge before us is to live a Spirit-filled life, a life of witness that is conducive to promote forces of hope.

2. The Second Coming of Jesus Christ

The crucifixion, resurrection, ascension, Pentecost, and the return of Christ are all interrelated. All these are to be seen within the framework of the "Christ- event." The Greek word that is very often translated to refer to the return of Christ or the second coming is *parousia*, which means active presence. According to Moltmann, to translate *parousia* as "coming again" or "second coming" is wrong, because it presupposes a temporary absence.[1] So the Christ who is going to come is the one who is with us; rather we are expected to be with him. As N. T. Wright reminds us:

> *In his appearing we find neither a dualist rejection of the present world but rather the transformation of the present world, and ourselves within it, so that it will at last be put to rights and we with it. Death and decay will be overcome, and God will be all in all.*[3]

The coming of Christ into our life is not to be seen as a once-for-all event at the end; but rather, we need to recognize his manifestations at different points of our finite life on earth.

In other words, the second coming of Jesus is to be understood as the fuller manifestation of Jesus. There are two approaches to the *parousia* in Christian tradition:

One: To felicitate Christ when he comes.

Two: To facilitate His coming to our midst.

The first approach is the Biblical literalists' approach which considers the second coming as something that is detached from the presence of Jesus in history. The problem with this approach is that the focus is to 'wait and see the Lord' when he comes! This is also an apocalyptic understanding of his coming in the clouds to receive the righteous. The second approach is more prophetic and historical in nature. The concern here is to take our discipleship seriously; to continuously examine whether our life is on the way of the cross unto the fullness of His Kingdom. What matters here is not the way we believe as to how he comes; but rather the task of God's mission that we are endowed with. Here, a constant review of our life of faith and discipleship are significant. Our aim should be discerning the presence of Christ, rather than waiting for his return.

3. Consequences of His Coming

a. God's Final Victory Over the Forces of Evil

One of the questions that is very often asked is this: How long will God allow the evil to flourish? Several believers, victims of unjust systems and fascist regimes, have died with this question in history. The Biblical answer, once again, is the resurrection of Jesus Christ. "*Then the wicked one will be revealed, but when the Lord Jesus comes, he will kill him with the breath from his mouth and destroy him with his dazzling presence*" (2 Thes. 2:8-9).

"Then the war broke out in heaven, Michael and his angels fought against the dragon, who fought back with his angels but was defeated, and he and his angels were not allowed to stay in heaven any longer. The huge dragon was thrown out-that ancient serpent called the devil, or Satan that deceived the whole world. He was thrown down to earth, and all his angels with him. Then I heard a loud voice in heaven saying: "Now God's salvation has come! Now God has shown his power as a King. Now his Messiah has shown his authority! For the one who stood before our God and accused our brothers day and night has been thrown out of heaven. Our brothers won the victory over him by the blood of the Lamb and by the truth which they proclaimed; and they were willing to give up their lives and die. And so be heavens, and all you that live there" (Rev. 12:7-12).

Evil has only temporal victory in this world. God who is just and righteous will not allow sin and the forces of darkness to say the final word. The question is whether we can choose life (Deut. 30:19) and it values over and against the powers of death at all levels.

b. The Fulfilment of God's will for Human Community

The Lord says: I am making a new earth and new heavens. The events of the past will be completely forgotten. Be glad and rejoice in what I create. The New Jerusalem that I create will be full of joy and the people will be happy... There will be no weeping there, no calling for help. Babies will no longer die in infancy, all people will live out their life span...People will build houses and live in them themselves – they will not be used by someone else. They will plant vineyards and enjoy the wine; it will not be drunk by others I will bless them and their descendants for all time to come (Isa. 65:17-25).

We have the same text with slight modifications in Rev 21:1-5.Perhaps, three dimensions are to be highlighted here:

- The symbolism of marriage (vs. 2)
- The vision of God's dwelling with humankind on earth (vs. 4)
- The consoling presence of God (vs. 4)
- In other words, in the fullness of time God's will for this created order will have primacy over everything. Our task is an earnest attempt to know and participate in the will of God as historical human beings.
- God's victory over the forces of death (vs. 4b)

c. The Consummation of Everything in Christ

With all wisdom and insight he has made known to us the mystery of his will, according to his good pleasure that he set forth in Christ, as a plan for the fullness of time, to gather up all things in him, things in heaven and things on earth (Eph 1:9-10).

In other words, the God intended purpose for creation is going to be a reality. Rather than making arrangements for the reception and felicitation of

Christ when he comes, our commissioning is to facilitate his coming in the midst of our historical predicaments, ambiguities and problems. This is possible only through our clear stances for his Kingdom and its righteousness.

4. How Should we Wait for the Return of Christ?

The three parables mentioned in Matthew 25 give us some guidelines. The parables talk about some of the essential Christian values in life, such as vigilance, faithfulness and compassion. The parable of the ten virgins points out that both vigilance and complacency can occur in the life of the church and only the vigilant ones can meet the Lord. In the parable of the talents the judging criterion is the faithfulness of the believers. The parable of the sheep and goats demands from us a life of compassion and the need to acknowledge the presence of Christ in the poor and marginalized.

The focus is clear: We cannot wait for the return of Christ in a passive, casual, inactive way. Rather, what matters is our creative involvement in the community, with clear perspectives. This has to do with the praxis dimension of Christian faith and hope. Two elements are common in all parables: human accountability and the judgment dimension of the Gospel. The early Church believed that the return of Christ would happen in their lifetime. When this did not happen, some were confused and some became complacent. Hence, these parables are considered as critiques of the mind-set of the early believers. Any predictions about the end of the world and the return of Christ would be meaningless. What we have in 1Thessalonians 4:13-18 is Paul's version of the manner of the return of Christ which was written in the context of kingship and within the framework of a three-storied worldview. Here, rather than the *how* and *when*, the *why* of the return of Christ is more important. Matthew 26:36 reminds us that even the son of man is not aware of that time. Hence, we must have the spirit of discernment not to be carried away by some of the so-called end time prophets and cultic leaders. As pointed out earlier, our primary concern should be the Kingdom of God as taught and lived by Jesus Christ to the extent possible in our life. What is required of us is conversion to this Kingdom (Mk 1:15) and our commitment to Christ on the way of the cross for the promotion of the values of the Kingdom. In other words, waiting for the return of the Lord should not be at the expense of our involvement in God's mission in the transformation of this world. What is of great importance is to be the agents of this creative hope in this world.

Finally, who can participate in the second coming of Christ?

Those who have committed their lives for Christ and his Kingdom.

Those who have lived on the way of the cross and for the establishment of thc Kingdom.

Those who are accountable, vigilant, faithful, and compassionate in life.

5. Challenges Posed by the New Generation Churches

Today there is a plethora of new generation spiritual groups in our villages and cities and several of our youth are under their influence. I do not propose to go into the details here. Rather than condemning them or threatening disciplinary actions against those who are with them; can we honestly ask the question as to why our youth are attracted towards these groups. Notwithstanding the fact that several of these groups have certain ulterior motives, the question is why do we miss our youth in the church, why don't they come to us for counselling or spiritual guidance and why do they find spiritual havens elsewhere?

This issue is quite complex which needs an in-depth study. As we are all aware, the spiritual needs of the youth are different. Some of them are emotionalists, some are radicals, and some are contemplatives, activists, and so on. Their problems have personal, emotional, and financial dimensions. In a permissive society, they are not at home with our legalistic, administrative, and rigid patterns. In addition to this, the high-tech style of operation of these groups, solid network, and above all new forms of music are all sources of attractions.

It is true that the preaching in most of these groups has a fundamentalist posture and with a made-it-easy-Gospel and it is doubtful whether these groups are really helping the youth in their search for meaning and fulfilment in life. But when the youth have their exam stress or other crisis situations in life, the leaders of these groups are with them with their panacea and truth claims. As pointed out earlier, to what extent can we make our parish or youth fellowship active and lively is the fundamental question here. Aare the clergy concerned about the youth presence in the parishes? How much of our time do we set apart for the youths?

Last, but not the least, we need to evaluate these groups in three areas: theological, historical, and pastoral.

One: What kind of a God concept do they promote? Does the Biblical God always reveal himself in and through miracles and signs? What is desirable here is thematic and in-depth Bible studies. What we have in these groups is over simplified answers to the complex issues of human life!

Two: The history of the Christian church tells us that there have always been counter movements and new generation churches. Some of these movements have had a revitalizing influence in the witness of the church. For example, the Confessing Church of Bonhoeffer in Germany and its unequivocal stances in the context of Hitler's Nazi regime. Similarly, the Reform movements under the leadership of Martin Luther in Europe and Abraham Malpan (Teacher) and others in Malankara Church were historical inevitabilities.

Nevertheless, the movement by Montanus of Phrygia who lived towards the end of 2nd century, popularly known as Montanism seems to be the spiritual-historical foundation of several of the present freelance, so-called charismatic, new generation churches. Tertullian, a gentile philosopher convert to Christian faith promoted this movement in Africa. Ecstasy, end time predictions, free – extempore preaching and administration of sacraments were the hallmarks of this movement. Though the church struggled with this for some time, it had a natural death. Though all characteristics of Montanism are not to be found in the contemporary new generation groups, we need to learn the lesson from history that self-righteousness and perfectionism are alien to the spirit of Christ.

Yes, Jesus is coming to our midst; but not necessarily according to our prescriptions, or the end-script prepared by the end time enthusiasts, or even the one given by Paul in 1 Thessalonians 4:13-18. Let me reiterate, his coming is totally unpredictable. What matters is not the manner of his coming; whether he comes again from heaven in the clouds or whether he fully manifests himself and we are able to discern his presence, is not for us to judge. Instead of making predictions, and only looking forward to meeting him in the clouds, let us conscientiously work with his Spirit to "make all things new."

10

Millenarianism, Messianism, and Rapture

The author is of the view that the doctrine of Millenarianism, though mentioned in Revelation, is not an essential Christian doctrine. Nevertheless, one chapter is set apart to study and examine the veracity of this doctrine as it's considered the most important text by the end time teachers and church groups. The attempt is to see the origin of the doctrine, and to place it within the life and ministry of Christ, especially his suffering messianism over against the political one in Judaism. Though there are a few apocalyptic references in the ministry of Jesus; he was mostly within the prophetic tradition. Here prophetic means concrete obedience to God as a historical human being. Similarly, the doctrine of rapture has had several ethical consequences in history. Hence, a re-examination.

The Millennium doctrine is the belief in the thousand year's reign of Christ and the redeemed on earth. Perhaps, John took over this thought from the Jewish apocalyptic tradition.

This is mainly derived from Revelation 20:1-6.

> *Then I saw an angel coming down from heaven, holding in his hand the key to the bottomless pit and a great chain. He seized the dragon, that ancient serpent, who is the Devil and Satan, and bound him for a thousand years, and threw him into the pit, and locked and sealed it over him, so that he would deceive the nations no more, until the thousand years were ended. After that he must be let out for a little while.*
>
> *Then I saw thrones, and those seated on them were given authority to judge. I also saw the souls of those who had been beheaded for their testimony to Jesus and for the word of God. They had not worshiped the beast or its image and had not received its mark on their foreheads or their hands. They came to life and reigned with Christ a thousand years (The*

> *rest of the dead did not come to life until the thousand years were ended). This is the first resurrection. Blessed and holy are those who share in the first resurrection. Over these the second death has no power, but they will be priests of God and of Christ, and they will reign with him a thousand years.*

Several attempts have been made to interpret this text. This is the key text that led to the doctrines which have fascinated many in Christian church history; the Adventists, Mormons and the Yahweh Witnesses. Surprisingly, this area is filled with end time predictions, speculations, visions, truth claims and what not!

To question whether Millenarianism is necessary is eschatology, Moltmann points out that the historical millennium is no and the eschatological millennium is yes. He makes a distinction between the historical millennium and the eschatological millennium as follows: "*Eschatological millennium is an expectation of the future in the eschatological context of the end, and the new creation of the world. Historical millenniu... is a religious theory used to legitimate political or ecclesiastical power, and is exposed to acts of messianic violence and the disappointments of history.*"[1]

The end time enthusiasts' literal approach to this text can be problematic because they fail to comprehend the apocalyptic language which is basically symbolic and allegoric. As pointed out earlier, ultimate truths can be communicated only in poetic, symbolic, and metaphoric language. In the mainline churches, very little attempt is made to interpret or reinterpret the text. As mentioned earlier, in the apocalyptic literature actual socio-political events are very often described in apocalyptic imageries such as war, natural catastrophes etc. We are confronted with certain hermeneutical issues here:

One: Would the 'ruling Christ' and the 'servant Christ' of the Gospels go together? For example, Jesus' admonition to his disciples who were arguing among themselves as to who is the greatest is this: "*Whoever wants to be first must place himself last of all and be the servant of all.*" (Mk. 9:35) The Lukan portrayal is more clear: "*Jesus said to them, the kings of the Gentiles have power over their people, and the rulers claim the title 'Friends of the people'. But this is not the way it is with you, rather, the greatest among you must be the youngest, and the leader must be like the servant*" (Lk. 22:24-26).

Two: What is the significance of thousand years?

Three: Why are the historical Jesus and Paul are silent about this doctrine?

Four: Has this ruler image of Christ led the church to justify Kingship and feudal Lordship in history?

Though a detailed exegesis of the text is beyond the scope of this section, a few comments are necessary.

1. Origin of the Doctrine of Millenarianism

This is mainly based on Jewish apocalyptic thought originated in Asia Minor. There was a development of this doctrine during the inter-Testamental period, especially during the Maccabean Revolt against the Seleucid Empire after the death of Alexander the Great in 2nd century BC. In 198 B.C, the Seleucids took over Judah and Palestine and promoted Hellenistic practices. Antiochus Epiphanus, the Seleucid Emperor wanted to convert the whole Jewish community to Hellenism. He even desecrated the Holy Temple of the Jews by putting an idol of the Greek god Zeus in 168 BC on the altar. (Dan11:31) This was challenged by a Jewish priest by name Mattathias in 168 BC. He challenged the Jews: "*Let everyone who is zealous for the Law and who stands by the Covenant follow me*" (1Maccabees 2:27). He formed an army and practiced guerrilla warfare. Finally, the Jewish army won the war and the Temple and the altar was rededicated to Yahweh. The celebration was for eight days and to this day, this is known as the celebration of Hanukah. According to some of the Old Testament scholars, this is the historical context of the origin of the doctrine of millenarianism.

We have reference to this in John 7:37, "*On the last day and the most important day of the festival, Jesus stood up and said in a loud voice: Whoever is thirsty should come to me and drink. As the scripture says: Whoever believes in me, streams of life-giving water will pour out from his heart.*"It is possible that during the period of Jesus, the Festival of Dedication became a mere ritual and hence the critique!

Some reflections in this regard can be found among the Patristics. While accepting the positive contributions of the Patristic Fathers (sic.), perhaps one of the controversial positions is in the area of millenarianism. Some of them were of the view that in the second coming, there is a reign of Christ with the redeemed for thousand years. This mainly arose out of the quest for the meaning of the second coming of Christ, and also the end times. A few among them even taught that at some time in the future all things will be restored in Christ, and even hell will come to an end. This is mainly found in Origen and also to a certain extent in Gregory of Nyssa and Gregory of Nazianzus.[2] The basic logic here is that God's love is so all embracing that He won't allow anyone to perish. But these Fathers, in a way, fail to acknowledge the power of human freedom, and the human urge to do away with God; such as agnosticism and atheism.

In Daniel 2 and 7 we have references to this doctrine. In Daniel 7:18 we read, "*The saints of the Most High shall receive the Kingdom and possess the Kingdom for ever.*"And in Daniel 7:27 we read, "*The Kingdom and dominion and greatness of the kingdoms under the whole heaven shall be given to the people of the saints of the Most High.*" These and several other messianic texts are to be seen in the context of the exile and the persecution of the faithful by Gentile emperors. Moltmann puts it succinctly: *They provide an answer to the besetting questions: why must the righteous suffer so much, and why do the godless have it so good? Where is God's justice?*[3]

One thing is clear; the persecuted communities were in deep crisis of faith. They had several existential questions and the exilic prophets struggled hard to keep their faith alive.

2. Messianism

The word *Messiah* in Hebrew and Aramaic means the "anointed." In the Old Testament the word was initially applied to the king. During the exilic period, the prophets oriented the hope of Israel on the future king. The concept of royal Messianism was developed after the exile. Cyrus, the gentile sent by God to deliver the people of Israel, is portrayed as the anointed of Yahweh in Isaiah 45:1. In the New Testament, one of the Christological titles used for Jesus is Christ which means Jesus is the anointed one.

This was mainly because of the Jewish hope which was alive in the formative periods of the New Testament. The early church saw in Jesus the promised Messiah of Judaism."Is he not the Messiah?" (John 4:29; 7:40-41) Reza Azlan, a New Testament scholar, sheds light on this trend as these self made 'messiahs' were branded in those days as "bandits." He says:

There was Hezekiah the bandit chief, Simon of Peraea, Juda the Galelian, his grandson Menahem, Simon son of Giora, and Simon, son of Kochba-all of whom declared messianic ambitions and all were executed by Rome for doing so.[4]

One of the questions very often asked is whether Jesus had the millennium belief and to what extent did he share and manifest this Jewish belief. Jesus was definitely a prophet of the *eschaton;* that which is ultimate. Apocalyptic imageries can be derived from some of his teachings and actions. For example, the imagery of Satan falling from heaven (Lk. 10:17) is reminiscent of Revelation 20:3. All his exorcisms are considered as the defeat of demonic forces and the signs of the rule of the Messiah on earth. In his triumphant entry into Jerusalem, the people shouted: "*Hosanna! Blessed is he who comes in the name of the Lord! Blessed is the Kingdom of our father David that is coming.*" (Mk. 11:9ff) In the New Testament, we have two notions of Messianism: Royal Messianism, the concept of the Messiah as the one who would come as a mighty warrior, and the Messianism of the Cross. Even though people saw in him the royal messiah, he did not want to be so. Among the disciples, Peter, who is considered the leader of the disciples saw in him a Jewish messiah. That is the reason why he attempts to stop Jesus from being crucified. Eventually Jesus had to rebuke him: "Get behind me Satan." (Mk. 8:33) For Jesus, the messianism of the cross was clear:

Then Jesus took the twelve disciples aside and said to them: Listen, we are going to Jerusalem where everything the prophets wrote about the son of man will come true. He will be handed over to the Gentiles, who will mock him, insult him, and spit on him. (Lk.18:31-34).

Rather than prediction-fulfilment, these are to be seen as the retrospective faith affirmation of the early Christian community.

The concept of the Kingship of Jesus is also significant in his context. This is considered by some as God's politics of truth in history. C. S. Song illustrates this point in the light of Jesus' encounter with Pontius Pilate, which was the culmination of the power conflicts that Jesus had with the religious and political forces of his time. As he observes:

This confrontation between Jesus and Pilate demonstrated the nature of God's politics with the politicians of this world, as essentially the transposition of power... Kingship for Jesus has to be established on the truth of God's creating and saving love.[5]

In other words, Jesus gives an entirely new perspective to the concept of Jewish Messianism; which even his own disciples failed to comprehend. For example, when he says in John, "'*When I am lifted up from the earth, I will draw everyone to me. In saying this he indicated the kind of death he was going to suffer.*" Here it is evident that the Jewish audience couldn't comprehend the symbolism used by Jesus. For them, the lifting of the Son of Man was nothing but the apocalyptic Son of Man in glory (John 12:32-34). But then the question is this: Why did Jesus allow the people to proclaim him as the son of David on Palm Sunday? *The crowds that went ahead of him and that followed were shouting:*

"Hosanna to the Son of David! Blessed is the one who comes in the name of the Lord! Hosanna in the highest heaven!" (Mt 21:9).

We are confronted with several questions here:

- Did Jesus arrange this event?
- Is it not a deviation from the concept of a suffering Messiah that he was trying to manifest?
- Did Jesus really need a public demonstration or a declaration of faith like this?
- Is it an attempt to make the event of Crucifixion sudden?

John interprets that Jesus was aware of the time to reveal himself as the suffering Messiah. As we see throughout his ministry, here also he is not overwhelmed by the crowd's praises! Rather, he knew for sure that he was moving towards the cross which is the definite consequence of his mission.

The Last Supper was an attempt to interpret his impending death on the cross. Of course, the church finds liturgical value in this. Notwithstanding its significance, this act of Jesus should not be seen as an attempt to give a sacrament to the Church. In other words, the events of Palm Sunday – Jesus' claim as the "son of David", the cleansing of the Temple, his prophesies regarding the holy city of Jerusalem – all these facilitated his journey to the Cross. Hence, the church's celebration of the Holy Communion is not just to commemorate or remember of what Jesus did on the cross, but to participate in his sufferings (Rom. 6:3ff). In other words, the Communion is not a *pooja* (a ritual act) pointing to itself and the Clergy are not to be seen as *poojaris* (priests) mediating the God's grace through the celebration of it. When we receive the Communion, we are also declaring our willingness to be on the way of the cross, unto the fullness of the Kingdom of

God. In other words, the response ought to be "Lord we are ready to be broken for you and your Kingdom." Well, it is beyond the scope of this section to go into the details of a sacramental theology here.

3. The Question of Rapture

This is considered as a supernatural event; the belief that the righteous will be taken up to heaven at the second coming and the unrighteous will be left over, or doomed. According to the end time teachers, our duty is just to wait and meet the Lord in the clouds! Just like Jonah who waited to see the fulfilment of his prophesy in Nineveh, the end time preachers would celebrate their rescue as well as the annihilation of the sinful. Attempts have been made to fix this doctrine in some of the sayings of Jesus, such as Luke 21.

But when you see Jerusalem surrounded by armies, and then know that its desolation has come near. Then let those in Judea flee to the mountains, and let those who are inside the city depart and let those who are out in the city enter it, for these are days of vengeance, to fulfil all that is written. Alas, for women who are pregnant and who are nursing infants in those days! For there will be great distress upon the earth, and wrath against his people. They will fall by the edge of the sword, and be led captive among all nations, and Jerusalem will be trapped under foot by the Gentiles, until the times of the Gentiles are fulfilled.

And there will be signs in the sun and the moon and the stars, and on the earth, distress of nations in perplexity because of the coming of the sea and the waves, people fainting with fear and with foreboding of what is coming on the world. For the powers of the heavens will be shaken, and then they will see the son of man coming in a cloud, with power and great glory (Lk. 21:20-27).

This portion is considered as the prophesied fall of Jerusalem to Roman army in 70 AD. In an unprecedented siege, the Jewish nation was obliterated; the Temple was set on fire and several thousands were captured by the Roman army. Here the author takes much of the older imageries of the Jewish apocalyptic thought regarding the 'day of the Lord' and attach them to the second coming of Christ.

The concept of rapture is mainly based on Daniel and Revelation.

Know therefore and understand that from the going out of the word to restore and build Jerusalem to the coming of an anointed one, a prince, there shall be seven weeks. Then for sixty two weeks it shall be built again with squares and moat, but in a troubled time. And after the sixty-two weeks, an anointed one shall be cut off and shall have nothing. And the people of the prince who is to come shall destroy the city and the sanctuary. It's end shall come with a flood, and to the end there shall be war, desolations are decreed. And he shall make a strong covenant with many for one week and he shall put an end to sacrifices and offerings (Dan. 9:25-27).

Different attempts have been made in history to interpret this text; especially the imageries used. According to some, as mentioned earlier, the passage refers to the events surrounding Antiochus Epiphanus (175-164 B.C). But some others would like to see these events figuratively. Some of the rapture enthusiasts also use 1 Corinthians 15 as an evidence for rapture. Though the concern of Paul here is the resurrection of the dead, and its basis is the resurrection of Jesus Christ, one of the basic tenets of Christian faith; the advocates of rapture would fit their doctrine into this too. Even 1 Thessalonians 4, which is considered as another rapture text, again is on resurrection. After having tried to respond to some of the issues among the believers in Thessalonica, especially with regard to the state of the dead, the coming of the Lord, etc., Paul concludes: "*Therefore encourage one another with these words*" (1 Thes 4:18). In other words, Paul's concern is not a rapture, but developing a credible faith and hope in our journey of faith.

In her thought-provoking book on Revelation, Barbara R. Rossing, sets the tone for a thorough revision of the concept of Rapture:

The central image of the book of Revelation as the nonviolent Lamb, who triumphs not by killing people, but by giving his life in love...Revelation's urgent message to us is of love, not escape.[6]

She also warns against the attempt to make absolutist political truth claims made in the light of Revelation. She considers this as the creation of the 'right wing' Christian end time enthusiasts, mainly in the United States. Challenging the story of *Left Behind* which contains mainly conspiracy, romance, violence, and Bible verses; she reiterates the message of the book of revelationas the story of God's pain-love and grace. As pointed out earlier, we need to rediscover the central message of Revelation; and the focus is the New Heaven and New Earth, Revelation 21, and the symbols of life in chapter 22. The prayer of the early, persecuted church, "*Come Lord Jesus*" (Rev. 22:20b) should go along with the prayer Jesus taught us to pray, "*Thy Kingdom come.*" The question to be asked is whether God's concern is to save a few and to destroy others, as the end time specialists preach; or the transformation of his created order.

4. Doctrinal Evaluation

Lastly, a few observations regarding this doctrine and the way it should be understood:

a. Purpose of a Doctrine

Doctrines are necessary. All religions and church traditions have doctrines. The question to be asked is why we need doctrines and what are we trying to do with our doctrines. Here the main difference between God and human beings is to be acknowledged. God is beyond the limitations of space and time and human beings are within those limitations. Hence, in order to talk about God and the relation between God and creation, we need Doctrines. But, we should also acknowledge that none of our doctrines can exhaust the meaning and mystery of God. All doctrines are derived in the light of the historical experience of the church. It doesn't mean that God is bound by any doctrine of the church. The emphasis here should be the faith experience of the community of faith; rather than a particular individual. Similarly, it should be acknowledged that God is not bound by any doctrine of the church or even what He has done in the past.

b. All Doctrines of the Church are Biblically and Historically Derived

Since Millenarianism and Rapture are only on the periphery of the biblical documents and also in the long history of the church; they should not be projected as vital elements of the Biblical truth. The need here is to distinguish between what is essential and what is non-essential. For example, the way Jesus challenges the Scribes and the Pharisees is note worthy, and in a way, normative:

"Woe to you scribes and Pharisees, hypocrites! For you tithe mint and dill and cumin, and have neglected the weightier matters of the Law; justice, mercy and faithfulness" (Mtt. 23:23).

As pointed out earlier, these teachings are emphasized in the Christian cult groups, and New Generation churches. Here, it can be pointed out that a teaching or a programme of our church should be evaluated in the light of the following:

- Does it motivate the believers in their journey of faith or in Christian discipleship?
- Does it enable the non-believers in the community to come to faith?
- Can we always emphasize a miracle-oriented faith in the light of the Gospel of the Kingdom of God that Jesus preached and manifested?
- Do we need to underscore the miracle of faith or miracle-oriented faith?

Here it is to be recognized that in such groups, very often, the faith of the believers are confused and the non-believers are made strong in their state of life. In other words, the criteria of evaluation of a church programme should be in the light of its proximity to the Gospel of the Kingdom of God and its values or its alienation from them.

c. Biblical Foundations of a Doctrine

The best way to assess a doctrine is to check its Biblical validation. Again, the question is *whether the Bible should be seen as a pattern of obedience or a blueprint for action*, as Dr. S. J. Samartha, the Asian theologian suggests. The Biblical literalists' approach is to look for texts, which would support their truth claims!

d. Historical Development of a Doctrine

No doctrine is an instant discovery. All doctrines were developed in the context of historical challenges and needs. No doctrine is the creation of a cult leader for his or her group. In other words, doctrines are to be seen within the framework of the early church, especially in the context of the persecution of the early church under the Roman Government. Some of them were heretical teachings within the church. For example, the Ebonite's emphasized the humanity of Jesus and negated his divinity and the Gnostics emphasized his divinity and negated his humanity. Some of the doctrines like the 'Lordship of Jesus Christ' had severe political consequences as it was against the political Lordship of Caesar in the pre-Constantine Roman Empire.

e. Defensive or Relational Doctrine

Very often it is said 'doctrine divides but service unites.' In other words, what is the validation of this doctrine in the wider community of faith? Among the early Fathers of faith, one group is known as the Apologetic Fathers, like Ignatius of Antioch, the martyr, and so on. Here '*apologetics*' is from the Greek word *apologia* which means defence out of strong convictions of faith! Tertullian, the Greek philosopher and convert to Christian faith said, "*The blood of the martyrs is the seed of the Church.*" In other words, Christian faith is not escapism or flight into another world, as the Millenarianism and Rapture enthusiasts advocate; rather, it is life with Christ or "costly obedience to Christ" as Bonhoeffer, the German theologian and 20th century martyr says.

Now the crucial question is this: Does this doctrine enable the faithful to be with Jesus in their journey of faith or does it indoctrinate them? Well, there are other Biblical symbols and imageries that we need to emulate.

The church's acknowledgment of the Kingship of Christ or the concept Messianism should not be used as a weapon to wage war against others, other religions, or communities, in defence of his Kingship. What counts here is God's politics of truth in history in terms of the promotion of values like freedom, justice, sacrifice, and so on. What we need is an unequivocal negation of all notions of triumphalism, royal or political messianism and instead an emphasis on Christ's servanthood, suffering and obedience even unto death. In a way, the history of the Bible is basically the history of two communities: the community of Israel and the early Christian community; how they obeyed and disobeyed God and God's concerns for this world.

Finally, let us be reminded that the concern of God in the Old Testament is how to redeem the world through the community of Israel; but they understood it as how God would redeem them. Similarly, in the history of the church, it seems that the concern of the Church is how we are redeemed through Christ; and not that how can we be agents of God's redeeming deeds in the world.

11

Eternal Life

The purpose of this section is to bring to the fore the fact that a dichotomy between life after birth and life after death is not Biblical and theological. Hence, eternal life is life with God in it's fullness; it begins here on earth. In other words, we can say, life includes death. There is an inner connection between life on earth and life in it's fullness in eternity. The task before the church is to promote the symbols of life at all levels, by promoting the search for alternatives in different realms of life. What is of great importance here is an integral vision of life; a life lived in authentic relationship with God, with other human beings and with God's creation.

Life includes death. Eternal life has to do with the depth dimension of life. It is life with God in its fullness; a state of life rather than a place to reach. Eternal life points to an element of transcendence in our present life. Very often, our framework is birth, growth, and death. But another approach is possible: life includes death. In other words, our life is a faith journey with Christ on earth, and the culmination of that journey is the fullness in eternity; in between, there is a physical death. Jesus Christ is the bearer and revealer of eternal life. It is not a natural deification or progress towards God through good works. In other words, the concept of eternal life challenges us to see the present in the perspective of eternity. Rather than escapism from the world and its realities, it gives us the urgency to transform the present in God's way.

Very often a dichotomy is made between life after birth and life after death. Some consider this life on earth only as a preparatory place for eternal life. Questions such as eternity, the meaning and mystery of life are discussed only in the context of death. Very often, in Christian spirituality, eternity is considered as the goal of life and life on earth as a necessary evil. This is a perverted understanding of the Biblical insights as well as the life and ministry of Jesus. The historical Jesus always took human life and human issues seriously. He always addressed human issues such as sickness, bereavement, marginalization, poverty, social taboos (e.g. leprosy), and so on. He confronted all these issues with ultimate concerns. His aim was not to save a few souls for eternal life. He never advocated negating this world for eternity. In an explanation of the *Jesus Way*, Aloysius Pierris says: "*He negated the revolutionary ideology of the Zealots, the sectarian puritanism of the Essenes, the self-righteous legalism of the Pharisees, and the opportunism and leisure-class mentality of the Sadducees.*"

In Malayam, a South Indian language, the term for '*eternal life*' is '*nitya jeevan.*' Here, *nitya* means daily and *jeevan* means life. In other words, Eternal Life has to do with our daily life. Similar words are *Nitya Vrithi,* which means daily needs, and *Nitya Nidanam,* which means sundry expenses. Hence, our understanding of eternal life should be in relation to our life here on earth.

The inner connection between life after birth and life after death is central to John's Gospel: "And eternal life means knowing you, the only true God and knowing Jesus Christ whom you sent." (John.17:3) In John's Gospel 'knowing' is not an intellectual comprehension, but rather 'intimacy.' This is closer to the Indian epistemology where the knower is also transformed in the process of knowing. We cannot make God as an object of our study.

1. Biblical Foundations

In the Old Testament, we don't have the concept of eternal life as we have it in Christian faith. Perhaps the only reference in this regard is Daniel 12:2, "*And many of them that sleep in the dust of the earth shall awake, some to everlasting life and some to everlasting contempt.*" In Judaism life is God's gift, value based life, life in God, etc. In Ezekiel 37, in the vision of the valley of dry bones, we have glimpse of this faith. The focus here is the renewal of the community through the work of spirit of God.

> The rich, young Jew came to Jesus seeking eternal life.
>
> *As he was setting out on a journey, a man ran up and knelt before him, and asked him, "Good Teacher, what must I do to inherit eternal life?" Jesus said to him, "Why do you call me good? No one is good but God alone. You know the commandments: 'You shall not murder; You shall not commit adultery; You shall not steal; You shall not bear false witness; You shall not defraud; honour your father and mother.'" He said to him, "Teacher, I have kept all these since my youth." Jesus, looking at him, loved him and said, "You lack one thing; go, sell what you own, and give the money to the poor, and you will have treasure in heaven; then come, follow me." When he heard this, he was shocked and went away grieving, for he had many possessions* (Mk. 10:17-22).

This is termed as the 'great refusal'! Here Jesus doesn't give any lengthy exhortation; rather he challenges him to amend his lifestyle and value system and to follow him. Jesus does not abandon the Law here; but he focuses on the need to go beyond the law. Even after having obeyed the Law, the person was deficient in his relationship with others. Here Jesus makes eternal life as something that is rooted in history and in relation to others. There is no shortcut to eternal life.

In a discussion on the relationship between history and eschatology, Paul Tillich brings out so powerfully the wider dimension of eternal life:

> *The ever present end of history elevates the positive content of history into eternity... Therefore nothing which has been created in history is lost... Eternal Life then, includes the positive content of history, liberated from its negative distortions and fulfilled in its potentialities... Life in the whole of creation and in a special way in human history contributes in every moment of time to the Kingdom of God and its eternal life. What happens in time and space, in the smallest particle of matter as well as in the greatest personality, is significant for the eternal life. And since eternal life is participation in the divine life, every finite happening is significant for God.*[1]

In other words, eternal life pervades the whole of creation and within its framework human participation in the divine life is possible. As we have seen earlier, the emphasis is the inner connection between life after birth and life after death.

John's emphasis is clear: "*I have come so that they may have life; life in its fullness*" (John. 10:10). As mentioned earlier, Christian faith gives us a view of life and also a way of life. This new perspective on life involves new orientation in life, new convictions, new commitments, and new relationships.

In our conscientious effort to follow Jesus, we are participating in the divine life. Here, we need to embrace a new set of values and a new scale of relationships. Eternal life means a life with God in its fullness. It has to do with the eternal significance of human life on earth. Jesus also challenges us to re-examine our priorities.

We cannot serve both God and Mammon (wealth). In some translations it is the 'idolatry of wealth.' In the contemporary globalized economy, where 'Mammon worship' is at its zenith, are we tempted to say no to Jesus and His Kingdom?

2. Affirmation of Life

There is a cry for life all over the world. We can discern a twofold nature of this cry. On the one hand, it is a cry of helplessness, agony, isolation, and desperation. For example, the cry of the HIV/AID victims, the old people, homeless people, orphans, and refugees. On the other hand, there is another cry of protest and hope. For example, the cry of Dalits, tribals, landless, migrant workers, refugees, fisher folk, and so on. Several of them are fighting for their genuine human rights, for their identity, for just wages, and so on. Our faith becomes significant only when we respond creatively and proactively to some of these cries. The Bible gives us several insights regarding the way in which God responded to these cries in history. It begins with God's question to Cain after the brutal killing of Abel.

> "*Where is your brother Abel?*" (Gen. 4:8) In the call of Moses in the burning bush we have this: "*Then God said, I have seen how cruelly my people are being treated in Egypt; I have heard them cry out to be rescued from their slave-drivers. I know all about their sufferings*" (Exo. 3:7). The mission of Jesus in its entirety was an extension of this response to the cry of human beings; the cry of children, the cry of demon possessed, the marginalized, the widows, the victims of an unjust socio-political order of Rome. Our task in our times is to discern the cries around us and to respond to those cries in the spirit of Jesus.

Here we have to distinguish between 'life' and 'physical existence'; 'human being' and 'being human.' There are three words for life in Greek language. "*Bios*" refers to life in general which includes all forms of life. "*Psyche*" refers to the emotional and relational dimension of life. It is also translated as "*soul.*" "*Zoye*" refers to the beyond dimension, the transcendent element and the sanctity of life. While the first two exist in nature which is part of God's created order, the third one has to do with the specificity of human life, which is God's image in the human. This element of life needs to be promoted through our life of faith. Faith gives us a new perspective on life – that life on earth is God's gift and what we make of it is our gift to God. Human life becomes meaningful only when it is at the service of God and human beings in the community.

3. To be an Eschatological Community

Life becomes authentic when we make it a vocation. A sense of vocation enables us to discern the sanctity and the 'beyond dimension' of life. Here we have to raise some of the ultimate questions such as *What is the meaning of my life?, What is the purpose of my life?, What should I do in my life?*, and so on. According to Paul Tillich, the famous Western theologian of the 20th century, "*That which concerns us ultimately is divine.*" As human beings we can work and so on.

The early church chose seven deacons to 'wait on tables.' This was in the context of an issue in the church; it was between the Jewish Christians and the Gentile Christians. We read that the Apostles took swift actions. They convened a common meeting, the issue was discussed, and a participatory decision was taken (Acts 6:1-7). Very often it is said that if you recognize a problem, you are halfway through its solution. The Apostles recognized the problem within the fellowship of the church. See the profundity of their decisions: "*It is not right that we should give up preaching the word of God to serve tables. Therefore, brothers, pick out from among you seven men of good repute, full of spirit and wisdom, whom we will appoint to this duty. But we will devote ourselves to prayer and to the ministry of the word.*" Here the decisions are collective and the Apostles are not imposing their decisions on the people. We also see recognition of the diversity within the fellowship of the church here. The Apostles recognize that there are people in the community who can 'wait on table'; perhaps more efficiently than them. Though this 'wait on tables' is traditionally understood as the distribution of food or financial matters; in the wider sense of the term it includes all so-called secular professions, such as teaching, counselling, nursing, medical work, social activities and so on. In other words, in all these areas we need people of good repute, full of wisdom and spirit. And academic excellence is not enough; it should go along with a life of commitment in the community. This shows how the early church ordered its life within the framework of eternal life. This is what we mean by an eschatological community.

Discernment of our vocation is human response to God's call in our lives. In other words, God would never impose His will on human beings. Rather, He inspires, motivates, guides, and leads. The challenge before us is always to opt for life or to promote the symbols of life at all levels.

4. Search for Alternatives

Abraham's call was to form an alternative community. Abraham is considered as the father of the faithful in three major religious traditions: Judaism, Christianity, and Islam. These communities are also known as Abrahamic communities. The task given to Abraham is to initiate a peoples' movement with God. In Jeremiah, the challenge is to be such a diaspora community: Seek the peace of the city. If the city has peace, you also will have peace (Jer. 29:7). The challenge here is to become real historical human beings and to stand for God's *shalom* which means peace with justice.

There are alternative searches in all fields all over the world such as alternative media, alternative medicine, alternative sources of energy, etc. This is due to human search for creativity and also the result of reverence towards life and a critique of the values of the market such as profit, competition, success, pleasure, etc. According to Konrad Raiser, "*Christian faith is a resistance movement against fatalism and resignation. When a person stops hoping death has the upper hand. Hope is the breath of life.*"

In a global context in which the search for alternatives and several of the micro-attempts have suffered a setback and people are very often carried away by the spiritual advertisement gimmicks and the mega–high tech programmers; the praxis dimension of Christian faith is significant. It is difficult for us to make a breakthrough. This doesn't mean that our efforts are fruitless. The Amish community life in USA is an eye-opener in this context. The Amish people are traditionally the descendants of Jacob Amman of the early Anabaptist movement in Europe who migrated to USA in 1600's due to religious persecutions. Today there are 220 Amish settlements in the 22 states of America; their main goal is to adhere to the principles of the early New Testament church. They lead an extremely simple life, travel on horses, eat the products of their own labour, respect and love each other.[2] We who live in a postmodern world are very often surprised at the Amish way of life. Notwithstanding all the criticisms that the Amish community is exclusive in nature, not open to the advances in the field of science and technology and so on, in the postmodern American society, the cohesiveness of the Amish life, their affirmation of life and higher values are commendable. As a visitor to this community in Lancaster, Pennsylvania, I was struck by the symbols of life within this community; their eco-friendly farming, reverence for life, contentment in life and above all, the negation of today's consumer products. There is definitely no 'sacralization of the market' within the Amish society.

How do we assess our own programs within the framework of the church? Is it in the light of success of a program? Completion of a project? Survival of an institution? or Faithfulness in what we do and commitment to Christ and his Kingdom? In order to confront the postmodern life style and its values, what we need today is fresh awareness of the value and worth of life in the community, the ability to distinguish between our needs and wants and also a deep sensitivity to those who are less privileged than us.

5. An Integral Vision

Relationship between life and eternal life (John 6:35,47) should be given due importance. In Christian spiritual circles often, a dichotomy is made between this world and the other world, life after birth and life after death. In the following words of Bishop Dom Helder Camera of Brazil, this dichotomy is brought to the fore: "*When I give food to the poor you call me a saint; when I ask why the poor have no food you call me a communist.*" But such a dichotomy is alien to the Biblical vision. Unlike the synoptic gospels, in John 6, the sign of feeding the five thousand is within the framework of Jesus' teaching about himself as the Bread of Life that is broken for the world. This has to with the qualitative dimension of life in Christ. We can experience this life only in our participation in the ushering in of the reign of God in and through Christ in the midst of all historical predicaments and uncertainties.

In the Eastern theological tradition we have an integral vision of life. Two Greek words are used for this state of life: *Theosis* and *Philokalia. Theosis* is considered as the highest spiritual goal of Christian life. Here transfiguration is not merely for Jesus Christ but for all of us. As in faith, in *theosis* also God takes the initiative and hence our response becomes possible. *Philokalia* is translated as higher spirituality or love for the good (*Adhyatma prema*) etc. Rather than a particular religious life or spiritual exercises, this has to do with a higher state of life. In a context of possessive love and selfish love in family life and church life, the question is whether we can inculcate some of these values? Simply put, the criteria of our spirituality is not our church membership, participation in Holy Communion or in spiritual gatherings but essentially what kind of people we become through all these?

The following prayer from WCC sums up the above insights:

> "God, come to us and journey with us so that we may walk in your grace and peace.
>
> Fill us with hope so that we may break through barriers.
>
> Inspire us on our ecumenical journey, making possible encounters and dialogue.
>
> Send your Spirit to strengthen us in our prophetic role of proclaiming liberation.
>
> May your Spirit be a gentle breeze when we need comfort and security;
>
> But let it be a strong wind when we are too settled and need to speak out.
>
> Let your life-giving peace come into our bodies and be expressed in action for peace between people, between churches, religions and between nations.
>
> May your transforming grace inspire us to join hands and declare the freedom given by your love.
>
> *Shower your blessings upon us as we journey on, announcing the good news of justice, caring and acceptance."*[3]

The basic question here is this: How do we assess the quality of our life? Is it in the light of who we are, and whose we are, or in the light of what we have? Eternal life has to do with the quality of our life; the values that we hold and the commitment and convictions that we have.

The culmination of our life is with Christ in its fullness. The question is whether we can create and support social forces that would facilitate life at all levels. In other words, eternal life is in relation to and fullness of our life on earth. Hence, the earthly life is neither to be glorified as such nor to be negated. Rather, it is to be lived in authentic relationship with God and with other human beings. The question here is whether we have the preparedness to be with God in His transforming mission in the world.

12

New Heaven and New Earth

This is the central theme in the book of Revelation which is adapted from the book of Isaiah chapter 65. Thelogically speaking; here the prophetic tradition is merged into the apocalyptic tradition. Here we have a cosmic vision and eschatology which emphasizes the inner connection between heaven and earth. Instead of taking the believers to heaven; we have the vision of heaven coming down to earth. This means that our task is to take our earthly life and the way of discipleship seriously. This also gives us the vision of a reconciled community, and also the creation of socio-political forces that are life-affirming and justice-oriented.

Two notions are found here: discontinuity and continuity. According to the notion of discontinuity, the new heavens and new earth have nothing to do with the present one. So first there will be total annihilation of this earth; then God will create his new haven and earth. Surprisingly, Biblical texts are quoted in support of this. One of the portions that is very often quoted is 2 Peter.

> "*Since all these things are thus to be dissolved, what sort of people ought you to be in lives of holiness and godliness; waiting for and hastening the coming of the Day of the Lord, because of which the heaven will be set on fire and dissolved and the heavenly bodies will melt as they burn! But according to his promise we are waiting for the new heavens and a new earth in which righteousness dwell*" (2 Pet. 3:11-13).

It is understandable that Peter is using apocalyptic imageries here. But, his focus is not to be misunderstood; that is, "the new heavens and earth in which righteousness dwells."

Some simple observations are to be made here:

- Would God annihilate His creation?
- What kind of a God do we see revealed in history and in the Bible?
- God is the one who created this *cosmos* (order, life) out of *chaos* (disorder, lifelessness); the one who is continuously trying to redeem it from its fallen nature; the one who sent his only son to save it through the cross and resurrection; the one who sent the Holy Spirit as the renewing Spirit; how can such a God annihilate his creation?
- As mentioned earlier, in the section of "Apocalyptic Literature," are the apocalyptic imageries to be taken literally?

In other words, it is always a fact of history that the emergence of the new is through pain, struggles, and sufferings. This is evident in all liberation struggles in history, struggles for justice and freedom, and so on. Even in the history of the early church, several of the faithful could challenge the idolatry of Rome with this vision of a new heaven and new earth.

Continuity, on the other hand, says that God who is the creator, redeemer is the one who creates and re-creates. His all embracing concern ever since creation is to renew the whole cosmos (Ps.104:30). Our task here is to be with His spirit in the process of this renewal. In other words, as mentioned earlier, the first approach is apocalyptic and the second one prophetic.

1. Paradise, Heaven, or Christian Utopia?

The concept of 'Heaven' is understood in a variety of ways in Christian faith: as the abode of God, the final destined place of the righteous etc. An equivalent of heaven that is found in the parables of Jesus is the 'Paradise' or 'Abraham's bosom' which has its roots in the Old Testament.

In the Old Testament, we have the concept of 'Paradise', which is part of the created order (Gen 1:1;Isa. 40:22); a place reserved for God. It is also called as a sanctuary (Ps.11:7). Yet, we also find the ideas that the heavens and the earth cannot contain God (1Kgs 8:27). The physical heavens serve as a symbol of divine transcendence and sovereignty over the world and history."The concept of heaven was developed in Judaism during the Inter-Testamental period; for example the different layers of heaven etc., which is not accepted in contemporary eschatology.

The word paradise is from the Greek word *paradeisos,* which means Garden. In some of the ancient religions in the Middle East, paradise was considered as God's garden. They also had the concept of the tree of life, water of life, medicinal fruits of the tree, and so on. These imageries are used in the story of the Garden of Eden in Genesis and in Revelation 21. Thus the theme of paradise had undergone several modifications in the Inter-Testamental period and in the Jewish apocalyptic writings. "*In the Apocrypha, …the paradise is an intermediary abode where the just shall be gathered together by God, to await the judgment day, the resurrection and the future life.*"[1]

In the New Testament, the words, heaven and paradise are used simultaneously. Sometimes, 'paradise' is identified as 'the highest heavens.' For example, Paul uses both these words in the description of his vision in 2 Corinthians 12:2-5.

In the Parable of the rich man and Lazarus, Jesus gives a new dimension to the concept of 'paradise' or 'Abraham's bosom.'

> *There was a rich man who was clothed in purple and fine linen, and who feasted sumptuously every day. And at his gate was laid a poor man named Lazarus, covered with sores who desired to be fed with what fell from the rich man's table. Moreover, even the dogs came and licked his sores. The poor man died and was carried by the angels to Abraham's side. The rich man also died and was buried, and in Hades, being in torment, he lifted up his eyes and saw Abraham far off and Lazarus at his side. And he called out, "Father Abraham, have mercy on me and send Lazarus to dip the the end of his finger in water and to cool my tongue, for I am in anguish in this flame." But Abraham said, "Child, you in your lifetime received your good things and Lazarus in the like manner received bad things; and now he is comforted here and you are in anguish*" (Lk. 16:19-27).

Here the rich man loses his 'paradise' for his lack of compassion; for his luxurious life, for being insensitive to the poor and so on. Here Jesus, the prophet of the *eschaton* underscores that there is a reversal of values, systems, and priorities in the ultimate valuing process. Here, the first becomes last and the last becomes first.

Lastly, a few words about Utopia. In 1516, Sir Thomas Moore published a book titled *Utopia*. He compared the social and the economic conditions in Europe with those of an ideal society on an imaginary island located off the coast of Americas. He called this fictional state Utopia; as something which could never exist. Karl Marx took over this concept in his *Communist Manifesto* and tried to make it historical. Leonardo Boff, the Latin American Liberation theologian, develops this concept in a section on *Personal and Social Utopia*. According to him,

> *Christian faith not only passes judgment on the utopia of others; it develops its own utopia for persons and society...It must seek the meaning of meanings, a framework calculated to establish humanity's definitive situation...the ultimate meaning of life can only be transhistorical.*[2]

All utopias are social dreams; the vision of a society that is just and humane; an ideal state of perfection; in Marxian terminology, a classless society. But in Marxian ideology, this is possible through human struggle, class wars, and so on.

Our task is not to replace the concept of 'heaven' with 'utopia' as it is a human construct; but to rediscover the meaning of heaven whether it has space for human historical involvement. I think this is possible as there is no dichotomy between the 'new heavens 'and 'new earth.' In other words, there should be interpenetration between the present heaven and earth. This can be considered as the transcendent dimension of our earthly realities and commitments.

2. Cosmic Eschatology

What is evident here is a cosmic eschatology. A question that is very often asked in this area is this: Is the new creation a spontaneous development or culmination of a historical process? Or, is it continuity or discontinuity with the present heavens and earth? Theologically speaking, rather than the culmination of a historical process, this is to be seen as the culmination of God's purpose for creation. Ever since the creation of this world, the Creator God has been engaged in its renewal in different ways. As the Psalmist reminds us:"*When you give them breath, they are created; you give new life to earth*" (Pslam 104:30).

In the concept of Sabbath Year in the Old Testament, the cosmic vision is brought to the fore:

> *The Lord spoke to Moses on Mount Sinai...when you enter the land that the Lord is giving you, you shall honour the Lord by not cultivating the land every seventh year. You shall sow your fields, prune your vineyards, and gather your crops for six years. But the seventh year is to be the year of complete rest for the land, a year dedicated to the Lord. Do not sow your fields or prune your vineyards...Although the land has not been cultivated during that period, it will provide food for you; your slaves, your hired men, the foreigners living with you, your domestic animals and the wild animals in your fields. Everything it produces may be eaten* (Lev. 25:2-7).

The concern for the land is significant here. That is given basically for cultivation as we see in the creation mandate: After having placed Adam and Eve in Eden, God said to Adam to till it and keep it (Gen. 2:15). Here, Eden is a state of life rather than a place, a state of perfect harmony and relationship. Rather than a day of rest, Sabbath is for the promotion of the forces of life at all levels. This is the concept of Sabbath that Jesus emphasized through his healings on Sabbath and the eventual saying: "Sabbath is for man, man is not for Sabbath."

Jesus always had a cosmic vision and he tried to manifest this in his life and ministry.

Hence, the environmental, ecological concerns not merely human activitists' concern; it's a Biblical, theological concern. We have a reference to this in Revelation.

> "*The nations raged, but your wrath came, and the time for the dead to be judged, and for rewarding your servants, the prophets and saints, and*

those who fear your name, both small and great, and for destroying the destroyers of the earth" (Rev. 11:18).

Very often, the commissioning given to human beings in Genesis is taken as the divine mandate to plunder the earth.

"So God created man in his own image, in the image of God he created him, male and female he created them. And God blessed them, be fruitful and multiply and fill the earth and subdue it, and have dominion over the fish of the sea and over the birds of the heavens, and over everything that moves on the earth" (Gen.1:27-28).

This text is very often quoted in support of the so-called 'anthropocentric approach': The logic that the whole created order is for human beings! There are different approaches to this topic. There is an interpretation that the Prophetic religions such as Judaism, Christianity and Islam are basically desert religions and hence not very nature-friendly. But, the mystic or nature religions such as Hinduism, Buddhism, and Jainism and so on, are more nature friendly. Having accepted the eco-friendly concerns in the mystic religions; a careful reading of the Bible would reveal several food for thought in this area. It is to be acknowledged that eco-theology is one of the major branches of contemporary Theology. Even the word, ecology is from the Greek root *oikos* which is translated as the 'household of God.' In other words, we are talking about God's household, the inhabited earth-it's whole biosphere. This is mainly in the context of different threats to life; the indiscriminate use of the land, unscientific developmental projects, pollution of water and air, deforestation, the extinction of several species, climate change and so on. Now there is a growing awareness that the concern for ecology is basically a theological concern, as we are sharing God's concern here.

One of the questions that comes to the fore very often is whether the whole created order is for human or vice-versa? The Christian faith has always been criticized by some of the environmentalists for its anthropocentric approach. A careful reading of the Biblical texts will reveal that human beings are for the created order.

Here it is to be noted that the vision of New Jerusalem in Isa. 65:17-25 becomes "New Heaven and new earth" in Rev.21:1-5.This is more inclusive and holistic in nature.

In 1982, the U.N adopted The World Charter for Nature, which says: "That the humans are inseparable part of nature, and that life depends on the uninterrupted functioning of the natural system. In the Christian theological field, there is a growing awareness of the human sin towards nature. Attempts are under way in the area of organic farming, nature friendly and green Parishes and so on. The slogan here is: Reduce, recycle, reuse. While accepting the positive contributions of all these developments, let me reiterate that our concern is not just nature; it is the whole creation, God's *oikos* which stands in need of renewal.

The entire Christ event should be seen within this framework. God's concern is not merely the salvation of our souls, as the early Gnostics thought; it is not salvation from this cosmos but in relation to it. God's realm of work is not merely nature, but the entire creation; the entire biosphere. Two notions can be seen in human approach to nature: Those who worship nature and those who plunder it. Both these are against the Biblical understanding of creation. Worship of nature is found in some of the tribal and primitive religions. Even the sun, moon, and other objects of nature are worshipped by several human beings. Though an attitude reverence to nature is at the core of Christian faith; a clear distinction is made between the Creator and the creation. Hence, worship is only to God who is the source of creation.

3. The Inner Connection Between New Heaven and New Earth

This is a central theme in Revelation. God is always in the process of creating life on earth. He wants us to be co-workers with Him in the promotion of life at all levels. He constantly challenges us to choose life (Deut. 30:19) over against the forces of evil, sin, and death in this world. The created nature gives us a vision of the spiritual significance of nature. The purpose of creation is not to return to the lost paradise but to march towards the new heaven and new earth (Isa. 65:17-25, Rev. 21:1-5). The Bible begins with creation and ends with new creation. In other words, the Bible begins with a garden (Eden) and ends with another garden, the New Heaven and New Earth. The purpose of incarnation of Jesus Christ is to make everything new by the restoration of all broken relationships within the created order. Bishop N. T. Wright points out: *The transition from the present world to the new one would be a matter not of destruction of the present space-time universe but of its radical healing.*[3]Peter gives us a holistic vision: "*But we wait for what God has promised; new heavens and a new earth, where righteousness will be at home*" (2 Pet. 3:13).

Two notions are to be negated here:

One: Glorification of heaven at the expense of the earth. This approach is found among the Biblical literalists. For them, the purpose of the church is to recruit people to heaven! Pentecostal and New Generation churches are competing each other as to who would make the maximum recruitment. This will lead to world negation and also this can be used as the basis for the church's disinterest in the affairs of this world. In the main line churches, this attitude is found in several of our convention songs and revival programmes.

Two: Glorification of the earth at the expense of heaven. Here heaven is considered as one's making in this world. This attitude is found in several of the secular ideologies. Though some of the secular ideologies such as Marxism, Gandhism, Sarvodaya of Acharya Vinoba Bhave, and so on have played significant roles in the transformation of communities; especially in the Indian context, any attempt to absolutize an ideology would be counter productive. Such absolutist tendencies have always had tragic ethical consequences in the community.

Samuel Rayan cautions us:

The immense progress we have made in science and technology has brought us to the brink of self-annihilation. We now have the power to wipe life off the face of the earth and blow up the globe in a few seconds.[4]

The question is whether a value-free approach to science and technology would be helpful in the forward march of humanity.

4. Integrity of Creation

Ever since the creation, the Holy Spirit has been active in its redemption. In Romans, Paul says that the whole creation is groaning for redemption (Rom. 8:22-23). In other words, the present creation will not be destroyed; rather it will be set free from all decay and chaotic forces. The whole concern of Paul is to demonstrate that the new creation is God's doing and the foundation is the death and resurrection of Christ.

The Biblical God is the God of creation. He creates and re-creates life on earth. Here is a reversal of some of the ancient West Asian god concepts that gods won't do any work and human beings are mere puppets in the hands of God. In the Biblical accounts a clear distinction is made between the Creator and the creation. The idea of creation as emanation from God is also negated here. The message is that the entire creation belongs to God and hence none of the created things should be idolized or worshipped. Moltmann borrows the word *perichoresis* from the Eastern theological tradition, to explain his concept of God's indwelling in his creation.

> *The new creation is defined through a new divine presence within it. The creator no longer remains over against his creation. He dwells in it and finds in it his nest. This makes of the new creation a sacramental world... The indwelling of God calls into being a kind of cosmic perichoresis of divine and cosmic attributes.*[5]

While underscoring Moltmann's ecological concerns, the question is whether there is an element of 'deification of the world' in this approach.

Creation is from chaos to cosmos (order out of disorder). The spirit of God always creates order. All chaotic forces are overcome here. The garden of Eden is not to be seen as a particular place but as an ideal state of life in which God, man, woman, and other creatures lived in perfect harmony but this harmony or the integrity of creation is broken due to human sin. Hence, sin is always reflected in broken relationships between God and man, between man and woman, and between man and nature (Gen. 3:1-19). In the vision of Isaiah, we see that in the messianic age these contradictions will be finally overcome and the harmony of creation will be restored (Isa. 11:1-10). One of the questions that comes to the fore is whether the whole created order is for man or vice-versa? The Christian faith has always been criticized by some of the environmentalists for its anthropocentric approach. A careful reading of the Biblical texts will reveal that human beings are for the created order. Here it is to be noted that the vision of New Jerusalem in Isaiah 65:17-25 becomes "New Heaven and New Earth" in Revelation 21:15.This is more inclusive and holistic in nature.

5. Symbols of Life

In Revelation 22:1-5 we have symbols of life such as the river, tree of life, fruits, and leaves of the tree with the power of healing of the nations, etc. A spiritual significance is given to life here. Biblical scholars tell us that in John's Gospel, the word 'life' is used instead of salvation. Jesus says: "*I have come so that they will have life, life in abundance*" (Jn. 10:10). The concern for life and its sanctity are to be seen in the early church's context of the Gnostic negation of life and the commoditization of life in our context of Globalization. In our consumeristic context, that which is saleable and marketable is of no value. Even in this 21st century in some of the villages in Tamil Nadu, female children are being killed as they are considered a liability for the families. Since the sex determination tests are banned by law in India, female foetuses are more or less safe in the mothers' womb. Modern science and technology offer several promises as well as threats to life on earth. The latest one perhaps is the COVID-19 pandemic.

The question that Moses poses before the people of Israel is more relevant now: Choose life."*I call heaven and earth to witness against you today, that I have set before you life and death, blessing and curse. Therefore, choose life, that you and your offspring may live*" (Deut. 30:19).

In Ezekiel 47, we have several alternative and life-giving images. Here the flow of the river is from the threshold of the Temple, greening the trees, and producing leaves and fruits, giving new life everywhere.

Always the choice between life and death is what makes our faith significant. The history of Judaism and Christianity would reveal that this has always been a difficult choice; a costly choice. Can we choose and promote symbols of life at all levels; within our church life and community life and also confront the anti-life or life negating forces.

In our attempts to define life and its worth, the Eastern concept of Transcendence is helpful. Transcendence has to do with the beyond dimension of life. M. M. Thomas gives a significant interpretation here. According to him, transcendence has two dimensions: transcendence in religion in terms of the ultimate and transcendence in terms of the future which is found in secular ideologies.

After having narrated some of the forces of death all over the world, such as sectarianism, obscurantism, and the divisive oligarchic regimes, Philip Woods, writes so tellingly: *Our times call for a prophetic imagination that can shape a different narrative to the prevailing one.*[6] He invites us to find symbols of life in some of the People's Movements across the World against fascist and oppressive regimes. In the prophetic imagination we always have counter narratives which are conducive to the forces of life at different levels.

6. Vision of a Reconciled Community

In the messianic prophesies of the Old Testament, the message of reconciliation is projected as one of the specific tasks of the Messiah. Unlike the Royal Messianism of Judaism, in Isaiah 11 we have the vision of a reconciled community.

> *There shall come forth a shoot from the stump of Jesse, and a branch from his roots shall bear fruit. And the Spirit of the Lord shall rest upon him, the Spirit of wisdom and understanding, the Spirit of counsel and might, the Spirit of knowledge and the fear of the Lord. And his delight shall be in the fear of the Lord. He shall not judge by what his eyes see, or decide disputes by what his ears hear, but with righteousness he shall judge the poor, and decide with equity for the meek of the earth; and he shall strike the earth with the rod of his mouth, and with the breath of his lips he shall kill the wicked. Righteousness shall be the belt of this waist, and faithfulness the belt of his loins. The wolf shall dwell with the lamb, and the leopard shall lie down with the young goat, and the calf and lion and the fattened calf together, and a little child shall lead them. The cow and the bear shall graze; their young shall lie down together, and the lion shall eat straw like the ox. The nursing child shall play over the hole of the cobra, and the weaned child shall put his hand on the adder's den. They shall not hurt or destroy in all my holy mountain; for the earth shall be full of the knowledge of the Lord as the waters cover the sea* (Isa. 11:1-9).

The symbols of life and vision of reconciliation here need special mention:

- Reversal of the role of Messiah from ruler to consoler, healer, judge, mother, etc.
- Alienation due to sin which is found in Genesis 3; such as broken relationship between God and human beings, human beings among themselves, and between human beings and nature are overcome.
- Justice to the poor and needy.
- State of righteousness and faithfulness.
- Knowledge of the Lord.
- Special care and protection for the children.
- Judgment of the wicked.

In Isaiah 65:17-25 the restoration of broken relationship and the renewal of creation are emphasized. In the prophetic vision of the new age, all the contradictions due to human sin are ultimately overcome. According to

S. Kappen, the new heavens and new earth are nothing but our heavens and earth divinized. What emerges here is a reconciled community where all the chaotic forces are finally transformed. The question here is how best we can manifest this hope in our historical action and options. Can the church create social forces which would be the first-fruits, the approximate historical manifestations of this prophetic vision?

7. The Task of Reconciliation

More than ever, the world stands in need of reconciliation. Ours is a broken world. This brokenness is reflected very much in the personal and social arena. Violence and terrorism are the twin evils which frequently seem to take humanity to the brink of a disaster. The tragic events such as the Ayodhya issue, bombing of the World Trade Centre, ethnic revolt in Sri Lanka and Kashmir, and the recent communal riots in Delhi have definitely created a cleavage in our world community which is yet to be healed. What looms large in our social fabric is often the so-called hate campaign. Here the law of revenge is projected as the final word. In this context, the world demands from us a rediscovery of the ministry of reconciliation. Reconciliation is basically the restoration of broken relationship at different levels. This is God's doing in the world. Ever since the creation, the Spirit of God has been active in the task of reconciliation-between God and man, human beings among themselves and between human beings and nature.

The Christian approach to war has always been a pertinent question here. How do we interpret the wars of the Old Testament? Very often the Biblical literalists justify wars because in the Old testament also the people of God had to fight several wars against the enemies of God! There are two schools of thought within the Bible.

One: The particularist school of thought

Two: The universalist school of thought

Some of the exclusive texts of the Old Testament portraying God as the 'God of wars' and so on are to be seen within the first school of thought. These texts are to be interpreted in the light of the self-understanding of the Jews as the only chosen people of God whose historical mission was construed as the annihilation of other pagan communities from the face of the earth. This polemical and confrontationist approach is not supported by the prophets. They emphasized the universality of God's love, God's preferential concern for the less privileged and the marginalized. Micah envisages a situation in which there won't be any war and violence. The prophet says:

> *He will settle disputes among the nations, among the great powers near and far. They will hammer their swords into ploughs and their spears into pruning knives. Nations will never go to war, never prepare for battle again. Everyone will live in peace, among his own vineyards and fig trees, and no one will make him afraid* (Micah 4:3-5).

The task of the chosen community here is to promote reconciliation and the furtherance of life and hope at all levels.

In other words, concern for reconciliation is basically a theological concern, an eschatological concern; God's concern for his creation. The efforts that are made all over the world for peace and harmony; through people's movements cutting across religious traditions are all God's concerns.

8. The Holy Spirit; Divine Energy for Renewal of Creation

The Spirit of God is the one who creates life; i.e., cosmos out of chaos (order out of disorder). The same Spirit is given to Adam when God breathed the life-giving breath into his nostrils (Gen. 2:7). This makes man/woman unique within the created order. Here it should be noted that this breath of life is given to the whole of humanity. This divine element within the human enables him to transcend himself and also to go beyond his earthly existence.

The Holy Spirit is always the empowering Spirit. Since human spiritual needs are different, the element of diversity and emotional expressions are all possible within the life of the church. However, we should not be carried away by today's TV evangelists and other emotional enthusiasts who would say that ecstasy is the only sign of the work of the Holy Spirit. The power from above is given to witness of Christ and His Kingdom (Acts.1:8).

The Holy Spirit is our divine energy, the spiritual fuel for an authentic life in the world. We cannot possess or privatize the Spirit. The Church does not have the monopoly of the Holy Spirit. The gifts of the Spirit are given to the believers for the edification of the community of faith (1 Cor. 12:7) and for the good of all. The Holy Spirit has been given to us by the grace of God. Rather than waiting for the Spirit to come again, what is of great importance is our availability for the work of the Spirit in and through us. We are to be constantly guided by the Spirit of God who empowers us, challenges us and opens up new possibilities in our journey of faith.

What we need is a relational life; a life of interdependence and his creation; a basic awareness that the created order "is an interdependent and integral whole... and environmental justice and social justice go hand in hand - as an earth ethic."[7]

A dichotomy between new heaven and new earth or between individual renewal and cosmic renewal should not exist in our life of faith. As individuals our task is to be sensitive to the still small voices within us and around us that are signs of hope for all. As mentioned earlier, the new earth and heavens gives us the vision that God's realm of operation is not 'up there ' or 'out there' but 'down here', with us. As we have seen erler, we are invited to turn to God because He has already turned to us. As Jesus negated all notions of fatalism and determinism such as political, religious and so on, our task is to be with him at the bleeding points of humanity. He doesn't want to be a cult figure of the church to be pleased by rituals and practices. His abode is no more in the heavens above; but "*his dwelling place is with us*" (Rev. 21:3). He is not to be sought in our church buildings but in the concrete situations of human life and its struggles. This is not to underestimate the value of the church and its sacramental life. But rather to emphasize the sacramental value and significance of life at all levels. Finally, the question is how we can be the instruments in God's historical process of renewal and re-creation; it is not how can we wait and see what God does in the end!

13

Last Judgment

The judgment dimension has to do with the nature of the Biblical God; who is active in the world, who is a demanding God, a just God. The sovereignty of God shows that human beings or hegemonic structures or institutions can't thwart the historical purpose of God for the created order. In Christian faith, unlike in other traditions, human beings cannot please God through rituals or sacrifices. God's anger is part of his saving grace and love. The criteria of judgment are whether our life is in compliance with God's plan for the world; a life lived in obedience to God, a life with a passion for truth and justice. We are not on our own; we are all accountable people, accountable to God and to the community.

This area of Christian faith is mostly misunderstood in our church traditions. In several of the conventions in Kerala, this used to be the last session where the preachers would threaten people with apocalyptic predictions and warnings. Always the emphasis is that the judgment of God comes after one's death. Now the question is whether the judgment element of Christian faith has a historical dimension. In the Nicene Creed we say: "He will come again with glory to judge both the living and the dead and of His Kingdom there will be no end."

Many have wondered the rationale for a judgment. N. T. Wright's words seem to be significant:

> *"In a world of systemic injustice, bullying, violence, arrogance and oppression, the thought that there might come a day when the wicked are firmly put in their place and the poor and weak are given their due is the best news there can be."*[1]

Some of the important dimensions here are the following:

1. Sovereignty of God

God is not to be seen as an absolute monarch, a sovereign ruler but as a loving father. Here the 'Fatherhood' of God is not to be seen as his 'maleness' but as the Person of God. Here it is to be noted that the Being of God is beyond human sexuality and there are masculine and feminine traits in the person of God. Some of the Biblical images of God are: Good Shepherd, Mother, Father, Liberator, Redeemer, Saviour, and so on.

One of the fundamental Christian faith affirmations is that "*God is the Lord of history, that the course of history is ultimately under God's control, and that God wills to bring the whole creation including human history to its fulfilment...because God is the Lord, God can carry out the divine will of love for the creation.*"[2]

The emphasis of Christian theology is not on the power and majesty of God, but on the love and grace of God. "*God so loved this world that whosoever believes in Him should not perish but have eternal life*" (Jn. 3:16).

As pointed out earlier, the basic question here is how to comprehend the judgment dimension of faith. God's love (agape) is the 'pain love of God.' In Jesus of Nazareth we have the embodiment of this love. The Gospels tell us that he loved his disciples till the end. Nevertheless, they continuously failed to reciprocate his love. Hence his admonition at Mount Gethsemane:

> *He went a little further on, threw himself face downwards on the ground and prayed. My Father, if it is possible; take this cup of suffering away from me. Yet, not what not I want but what you want. Then he returned to the three disciples and found them asleep; and he said to Peter: How is it that you three were not able to keep watch with me even for one hour?* (Mt. 26:39-40).

Biblical scholars point out that *agape* in the New Testament is used as a verb. In other words, love in Christian faith is not an emotion but an action. This love of God has two dimensions: caring dimension and judging dimension. In other words, judgment is part of God's love.

2. The Wrath of God

Judgment also points to the fact that human beings can eternally be rebellious to God and his plan for the world. In the Bible, we have several references to the love and wrath of God. Even though human beings with all their scientific and technological skills cannot thwart God's eternal plan for the world; they can disrupt and pervert it through sin. The Biblical God becomes angry when his children deliberately choose the way of evil and death. Hence, he threatens with punishment when his will and purpose are violated continuously.

In Prophetic books we have several references to God's wrath. A few are given below:

> *Woe to you who join house to house... Woe to those who tug at guilt with cords of perversity... Woe to those who call evil good and good evil... Woe to the champions at drinking wine. To those who acquit the guilty for bribes and deprive the just man of his rights! Therefore the wrath of the Lord blazes against his people; He raises his hand to strike them* (Isa. 5:8-25).

These are the words of Nahum regarding the Lord's coming judgment against Nineveh:

> *A zealous and avenging God is the Lord, an avenger is the Lord and angry. The Lord brings vengeance on His adversaries; and lays up wrath for His enemies. The Lord is slow to anger, yet great in power, and the Lord never leaves the guilty unpunished. In hurricane and tempest is his path, and clouds are the dust at his feet. He rebukes the sea and leaves it dry, and all the rivers he dries up. Withered are Bashan and Carmel, and the blossom of Lebanon fades. The mountains quake before him, and the hills dissolve; the earth is laid waste before him, the world and all who dwell in it. Before his wrath who can stand firm, and who can face his blazing anger? His fury is poured out like fire, and the rocks are rent asunder before him* (Nahum 1:2-6).

The focus is clear. Human sin adversely affects the ecological balance. In other words, these are cosmic effects to the anger of God. We have a similar passage in Jeremiah:

> *The children gather wood, their fathers light the fire and the women knead dough to make cakes for the queen of heaven while libations are poured out to strange gods in order to hurt me. Is it I whom they hurt, says the Lord; is it not rather themselves ...? See now ... my anger and my wrath will pour out upon this place, upon man and beast, upon the trees of the field and the fruits of the earth; it will burn without being quenched"* (Jer 7:18-20).

But in Zechariah's vision we have a new aspect of the anger of God ripening to mercy:

> *The angel of the Lord spoke out and said: O Lord of hosts, how long will you be without mercy for Jerusalem and the cities of Judah that have felt your anger these seventy years?*
>
> *To the angel... the Lord replied with comforting words, and the angel said to me, proclaim: Thus says the Lord of hosts; I am deeply moved for the sake of Jerusalem and Zion, and I am exceedingly angry with the complacent nations; whereas I was a little angry, they added to the harm. Therefore*

> *I will turn to Jerusalem in mercy...My cities shall again overflow with prosperity; the Lord will again comfort Zion and again choose Jerusalem"* (Zec. 1:12-17).

In the New Testament we have similar references from the life and ministry of John the Baptist and Jesus. For example, his question to those who came to him: "*Who told you to flee from the wrath to come?*" (Mt. 3:7). There are several such passages in Matthew, especially Jesus' admonition to the Pharisees and Sadducees: "*How terrible for you teachers of the Law and the Pharisees! You hypocrites! You lock the door to the Kingdom of heaven in peoples' faces and you yourselves don't go in, nor do you allow in those who are trying to enter!*" (Mt. 23:13-14). There are several similar condemnations of the Jewish hierarchy and their perfectionism and legalism in Matthew 23.

In Mark 3, he looks around at them in anger (vs.5). A significant proclamation of Jesus in John's Gospel is this: "*Whoever disobeys the son will not have life, but must endure the wrath of God*" (Jn. 3:36). Mark narrates two occasions when Jesus becomes angry or indignant.

> *He said to the man with the withered hand, "Stand in the middle." Then he said to them, "Is it against the Law on the Sabbath day to do good, or to do evil; to save life or to kill?" But they said nothing. Then grieved to find them so obstinate, he looked angrily around at them...* (Mk 3:2-5).

People were bringing little children to him, for him to touch them. The disciples turned them away, but when Jesus saw this he was indignant (Mk. 10:13-14).

Human insensitivity to suffering is challenged here. Jesus becomes angry when the rituals and religious laws were not promoting values and when they stand in the way of life and its values. His wrath is his No to all systems of anti-human and anti-life elements. In Paul's letters, the concrete forms of divine wrath are idolatry, sexual immorality, and greed, and murder, lack of loyalty, affection and unrighteous life. Our community life and church life are replete with all these and many more vices. What thrives in our times is the sex industry, oppression of the weak, the widows and orphans, injustice in our church structures and so on. In spite of the efforts of the legal services to the poor, the question is whether they would get justice from the judiciary. Several of our judges like the Late Justice V. Krishna Iyer have pointed out this issue. Rather than making truth claims, can the churches vindicate the claims they make for themselves such as the one, holy, catholic, and apostolic church?

We are confronted with certain issues here:

- Is there a distinction between the God of the Old Testament and the God of the New Testament? It is very often seen that in the Old Testament God is a zealous one, who takes vengeance and punishes people, whereas in the New Testament we have a God who is the embodiment of love and compassion.

- How does God punish a community in its entirety for the sins of a few?
- Are these faith attempts to create fear among the people to keep them faithful?
- What is the relevance of this God concept in an age of democracy and human freedom? According to Mar Chrysostom Metropolitan, human freedom includes the freedom to deny and even disobey God!
- In an age of science and technology where the autonomy of human reason is the norm, can we hold this God concept?
- Are these attempts to impose monotheism in a context of polytheism?

The sins which provoke Yahweh to anger are mainly two: idolatry and injustice. These two are therefore the main targets of his wrath, the principal evils of which the fire of his rage seeks to burn up, and from which the floods of his fury seek to purify the earth.[3] If so, can we identify the revelation of God's wrath in the context of genocides, ethnic cleansing, war industry, support to dictatorship and fascism, violation of human rights, especially the right to know and so on! How do we account for the silence and the neutrality of the churches at the bleeding situations of human life? A few of our church leaders in Kerala are facing criminal charges: one is a nun rape case, another a corruption case, and so on. Recently a Bishop was detained in his office in Delhi for several hours by the members of the church demanding just and corruption-free governance in the Diocese! How does God's wrath reveal in all these? While accepting the fact that a perfect system may be difficult; the question is whether we can make situations that are more conducive to justice and values in our church life.

Revelation 6 talks about the anger of the Lamb:

> *Then the Lamb broke open the fifth seal. I saw underneath the altar the souls of those who had been killed because they had proclaimed God's word and had been faithful in their witnessing. They shouted in a loud voice "Almighty Lord, Holy and true! How long will it be until you judge the people on earth and punish them for killing us?" Each of them was given a white robe, and they were told to wait a little while longer, until the complete number of their fellow-servants and brothers had been killed, as they had been.... Then the kings of the earth, the rulers and the military chiefs, the rich and the powerful and all other men, slave and free hid themselves in caves and under rocks on the mountains. They called out to the mountains and to the rocks, fall on us, and hide us from the eyes of the one who sits on the throne and from the anger of the Lamb!* (Rev. 6:9-16).

John's vision is clear: Christ the Lamb is the only one who is capable to break the seals. Christ is not just a silent spectator of events; he confronts the socio-political powers who oppress his people. With his holy anger he defeats the agents of the oppressive regime. Here the cry of the victims is reminiscent of the cries of many faithful in the Old Testament. "*From the depths I call to you, Yahweh, Lord, hear my cry*" (Ps.13, 130). We have several examples of this cry of those tortured for their convictions in different situations in history. The brutal killing of the Australian missionary Graham Stains and his sons by the Hindutva fundamentalists in Orissa is a case in point. Here the plea of the victims is not to be construed as a call for personal vengeance which is against the Gospel of Jesus Christ. "*In the context of the whole message of Revelation, it is rather a plea that justice be done: God's justice which takes account of the sacrifice of the Lamb while judging all evil powers, God's justice which vindicates the victims and accomplishes the design of salvation.*"[4]

The anger of God (wrath) comes out of God's nature and God's expectations about humankind. "*What he requires of us is this: to do what is just, to show constant love and to live in humble fellowship with God*" (Micah 6:8). In the Greco-Roman god concepts, people had to please god through prayers and sacrifices. Even in the Old Testament we have such notions. But the prophetic corrections are noteworthy. In the words of Samuel Rayan, the Indian Jesuit scholar, "*We have to celebrate the anger of God in history.*" Good parenting is considered as authoritative rather than permissive or authoritarian. Our counsellors tell us that authentic parenting includes freedom of children, as well as the boundaries set for their actions. So, the task of the parents is to be with their children, without intruding into their personhood so that they grow as matured human beings. Similarly, God gives us freedom and he also sets limits within that freedom. In other words, real freedom is always the freedom with responsibilities and within limits. This is basically the freedom to do what is good and the freedom to promote life and relationship. No one on earth has the freedom to do evil. As parents have expectations about their children, God has a dream for all of us (See Bishop Desmond Tutu's book in this area: *God has a Dream*). When children continuously make wrong choices and disrupt family life, good parents would definitely intervene and make corrections or perhaps, on certain occasions give reformative punishments. Well, the element of Judgment should be seen along those lines. Here judgment comes out of God's concern for his creation. It is not punitive but reformative in nature. There are references in prophetic books such as Jeremiah, in the context of the disobedience, exile, and the suffering of the people Yahweh says: "*But if you will not listen, my soul will weep in secret for your pride; my eyes will weep bitterly and run down with tears, because the Lord's flock has been taken captive*" (Jer. 13:17). And after having given punishment to his people, God is in pain; his heart yearns for those who go astray and he cries in secret (Jer. 31:20). Again, if a human analogy is used, no normal parents would have peace of mind after punishing their children. Punishment is always painful. But that is essential for renewal as in the case of a surgery.

Jesus' analogy of the vine and the branches sounds relevant in this context: "*I am the vine and my father is the gardener. He breaks off every branch that doesn't bear fruit, and he prunes every branch that bears fruit*" (Jn. 15:1-3). The pruning process is painful but that is essential for growth and fruit bearing. In other words, as Moltmann points out:

> *The Last Judgment is not a terror. In the truth of Christ, it is the most wonderful thing that can be proclaimed to men and women. It is a source of endless consoling joy to know, not just that murderers will finally fail to triumph over their victims, but that they cannot in eternity even remain the murderers of their victims.*[5]

The theme 'wrath of God' reminds us that the Biblical God is a zealous God, a demanding God, who seeks justice and righteousness, faithfulness in our systems and institutions.

3. The Criteria of Judgment

It is not church membership or a life of piety but whether we are compassionate to the needy that matters. "*Then the king will say to the people on his right, come you that are blessed by my Father!...I was hungry and you fed me, thirsty and gave me a drink. I was a stranger and you received me in your homes, naked and you clothed me; I was sick and you took care of me; in prison and you visited me*" (Mt. 25:34-36). We can look at this text in two ways: a benevolent master's approach or a suffering servant's approach.

The first one is the common charity method. The attempt to take care of the victims of unjust social orders. They have the Biblical rationale in the saying of Jesus, in his conversation with those who scolded Mary after her anointment of Jesus at Bethany: "*You will always have the poor with you, and whenever you want, you can do good for them*" (Mk. 14:6-7). Does it mean that Jesus is romanticizing poverty? Or, all human efforts to transform and liberate the poor are meaningless? One of the interpretations given by S. Kappen goes like this: So long as you have the structures of sin within your community, you will have the poor with you. This author is reminded of the Golden Jubilee programme of the Kumbanad Mandiram, a destitute Home in Kerala. Sri.Kadammanitta Ramakrishnan, a leftist poet and politician was there to give a felicitation. In his brief message he said: I hope and pray that all the destitute homes and orphanages in our state be closed as early as possible! In other words, he was driving home the question as to why do we need destitute homes and orphanages. This is because our system is not just. Well, do we expect more people to come to these homes so that we can take care of them? This may be too idealistic a thinking: a just system without poor and needy.

The suffering servant approach is slightly different. There is no condescension here. Though there are attempts to take care of the victims of oppressive and unjust social systems, the concern here is not to glorify such systems but to transform them. The truth is that most of our programmes and projects are with a 'Benevolent master's mindset.' This is mainly because we are not in a position to challenge the unjust social systems. As Bishop Dom Helder Camera of Brazil points out: *When I give food to the poor, you call me a saint. When I ask why the poor have no food, you call me a communist.* The judgment of God in the book of Revelation is in the light of the obedience of the faithful till the end.

4. Human Accountability to God and Community

All human beings are ultimately accountable to God and to the community. In other words, we are not on our own and our destiny is not in our hands. This dimension of human life; though difficult for many in the church and outside, would make us humble and also make us aware of our finitude. Contrary to this, the modern mindset seems to be this: I am a self-made man/woman and my destiny is in my own hands. It seems God comes here as an intruder into human privacy and freedom!

Yet, God doesn't condemn anyone. God basically judges human sin which is understood in a variety of ways such as disobedience, misuse of freedom, alienation from God and his creation, humanity's break with the Covenant, and the perversion of the *imego Dei* and so on. The widespread attitude of relativism in our contemporary culture is an issue to be addressed in any discussion on the concept of sin.

> "*On the one hand, relativism has the positive potential of acknowledging the specific, contextualized predicament of the other. Yet, on the other hand, relativism seemingly makes it difficult to make any absolute judgments of value. When grappling with the question of how to be human in relation to others, relativists answer that all options are viable, depending on situations; there is no one right or just course of action.*"[6]

The basic question here is whether human beings are slaves of their situations. Or do we have mastery over them? Would the Image of God within us allow us to be so? It is as if relativism can promote an attitude of 'sin boldly no matter what' kind of approach which has tragic ethical consequences in the community.

The love and grace of God are very often taken casually in Christian life. Death does not separate us from the love and grace of God. The grace of God is totally unpredictable. God has his own ways of accomplishing his plan of salvation. No one is excluded from this salvific plan of God. In other words, God's dealings with human beings are not condemnatory but redemptive in nature. Here 'heaven' and 'hell' are not to be understood in the categories of space but as the culmination of two states of life and two ways of life on earth; as the inevitable end of our choices in life. God does not impose his will on anyone; rather, he motivates us to make right choices in life.

This approach can lead to some issues. Does it mean that even after death we are given a chance to repent and to turn to God? If so, one can succumb to the temptation to take this life and faith for granted. Martin Luther, the reformer of the church in Europe, vehemently challenged the concept of purgatory and the sale of Indulgences, which were prevalent in the Roman Catholic Church as after-death rites in those days.

The New Testament references to Jesus' descent into the Hades are very often projected as the justification here.

> "*For Christ also suffered once , for the righteous and for the unrighteous, that he might bring us to God, being put to death in the flesh, but made alive in the spirit, in which he went and proclaimed to the spirits in prison, because they formerly didn't obey...*(1Pet 3:18-20).

> "*For this is why the Gospel was preached even to those who are dead, that though judged in the flesh the way people are, they might live in the spirit the way God does*"(1 Peter 4:6).

Here it should be remembered that the purpose of the Biblical writers is not to teach astronomy. Rather, their intension is to bring out the eternal relevance of Jesus Christ within the divine salvific plan of God vis-à-vis the worldview of those days.

The early Church had before them the following faith (theological) issues:

One: What is the ultimate future of those who did not have an opportunity to listen to the Gospel of Jesus Christ? How would God deal with them? Are they condemned forever or do they have an occasion to listen to the Gospel and thereby a second chance to repent in the light of the all-pervading grace of God?

Two: Where was Jesus after his crucifixion and resurrection? Perhaps this is also reminiscent of the pertinent question of Jesus at Caesarea Philippi: Who do you say that I am? According to the faith of the church, Jesus didn't die a natural death. His whole life and ministry was within the salvific will and divine plan of God.

These questions are indeed Christological in nature. We have the faith response of the early church in the story of Jesus' descent into the Hades. Now the question to be asked here is not whether Jesus did really go to the Hades after his death or how did he go there and so on, but rather what is the meaning of this belief of the early church and what message does it communicate to us who hold another worldview.

Though the Mar Thoma Church uses the ancient Eastern liturgies, the church does not practice the prayers for the dead and prayers to the dead perhaps for non-theological reasons such as the degeneration of those practices during the pre-reformation times in the Malankara Church in Kerala. Here the following subtle words of the Metropolitan Mar Chrysostom sound contextual:

> *Theologically speaking, praying for the dead may have some justification. Though we are not sure of our immediate status after death, we believe that death cannot separate us from the love of Christ. What went wrong*

> *however was not so much the theology as the practice of praying for the dead- a practice which deteriorated to such an extent that people believed that irrespective of how a person led his life, the priest could, through appropriate rituals, ensure eternal life for him.*[7]

While acknowledging the question regarding the efficacy of praying for the dead, the status of the dead and so on; the question is whether the Eastern concept of the church as the community of the living and the dead can be ignored in our theological articulations.

Christian faith becomes meaningful only when we recognize God as our loving Father; a reciprocal love or love in action is what makes our lives significant. He is also a just and demanding God; the one who would like to see his creation live in peace and justice at all levels. The wrath and judgment of God is part of his demanding love; his concern is for a community that is justice oriented. Unlike some of the other religious traditions where God can be pleased through sacrifices and rituals; what matters in Christian faith is the way we manifest God's concerns in our life on earth. Instead of being afraid of the final judgment, our response should be a life of faithfulness and accountability.

14

Graceful Living, Ageing and Dying

The first part of this chapter points out that the human body is not a consumer product as it is very often construed in the market ideology; rather an inevitable part of human entity in the community. Unlike the early Gnostic teachings, all human bodily functions affect the human entity. Christian life on this earth is a reality; and ageing and death are also realities. We do very little study and reflection on the meaning and mystery of death. Very often it is done only in the context of a burial. We have to continuously add life to our years and not just years to life. Graceful living and graceful death are inter-related.

Though this section is on the Christian understanding of life and death, a few observations on this topic from other traditions are helpful. Let me cite three examples.

First, this author remembers having read the last article written by Vaikom Muhammed Basheer, a well-known Malayalam novelist who is known for his down-to-earth literary style. In his eighties, he had an intuition that he would die soon. He took out his pen and started writing on the meaning of life and death. Towards the end, he thanks everybody who supported him in his life, especially in his literary work. He thanks his family members, his neighbours, his pets, and fruit trees in the courtyard. Then he says, "I have not done so much that you will always remember me; perhaps, through my writings, you may remember me for some time. Now I have started my journey into the realm of death; the realm of Allah." Finally, he says, I have died…and his pen falls down, as the family members reported, and he died peacefully!

Second, Guru Nithya Chaithya Yathi, a Hindu scholar and visionary narrates the following experience in one of his books: Once he was in Patiala, in North India, walking on the streets to one of his friend's home. On the way, he met a man who came with a request to go with him and pray for his dying master. Soon he found a 70-year-old person, in a palatial building who was about to die. He was laid on white linen and was lying helplessly on the floor. Guru waited near the gate and asked the gate keeper, what is happening inside. He said that one person is dying and the *poojaris* (Hindu priests) are offering the last rituals. Yathi went inside and sat near the person. Suddenly, the dying person took Yathi's hand and said, "Guru, will you forgive my sins? I want to live!" Yathi, says he was initially hesitant, as he knew only Jesus could do that; but thinking it was the request of a dying person, he replied, "Yes. You will not die; you will live!"And he says, he doesn't know who made him say that. Immediately he left the place. After several years, Guru Yathi was on a pilgrimage to Haridwar and one Swami came and knelt before him and asked the Guru, "Do you recognize me? I am the person you met in Patiala several years ago; about to die and you gave me the assurance that I will not die! Ever since that day, I am living a new life! As Jesus said to the rich man, '*Give all your money to the poor, and follow me*', *I left everything and I am walking a new way*."[1]

What we see in this example is the passion for life and also a life lived in the community with a definite purpose. This is not to say that Nitya Chaitanya Yathi had divine powers. He also says in his book that he had that kind of an experience only once in his life. I had several opportunities to listen to him; and he never made any such claims.

Third, the life of John Abraham, a famous Malayalam film director and a secularist. He was always afraid of death; to the extent that if he receives the news of someone's death in his village or family, he wouldn't sleep or eat his food for several days!

A detailed analysis of the meaning of life and death in different traditions is beyond the scope of this section. Nevertheless, it is to be noted that if we are reconciled with death, life will be smooth. Similarly, if life is lived in good relationship in the community; if you are owned by others and vice versa, death won't be a fearful and inevitable tragedy.

A few insights in this area are given below:

1. Theology of Human Body

The early Christians were ridiculed by Celsus, the Hellenistic philosopher, as a *philosomatic* (body loving) people. For Plato body is mortal and soul is immortal. But for Aristotle, "Nothing human, not even the soul, survives the grave." The significance of human body is to be seen in the context of two notions: the Greek notion of the negation of body as evil and also the contemporary commoditization of body as a marketable one. In Hinduism also human body is considered as the seat of all evil: (Eg. *kama*, *krodha*, and *moha*-which means licentiousness, anger, and desire respectively).

a. Greek View of Human Body

In the Greco-Roman world human body was considered as the seat of evil. The early Christian Gnostics, who were influenced by the Greek philosophical dualism with its concept of two-layered man, negated the human body and bodily functions for the liberation of the soul. This value and worth of human body is to be cherished in our context of the commoditization of body. It seems as if human body is considered as a commodity in today's market and its advertisements. Here we are confronted with two extreme positions: First, the negation of the body and perhaps, the attitude that the body is an inevitable evil and thereby the human bodily functions as opposed to the work of the spirit in spiritual circles. And secondly, the absolutization of the body and bodily functions, which is the tendency to satisfy only the human physical needs through new consumer products in the market.

In the Gnostic spirituality, the emphasis was on the immortality of the soul. Hence, the devotees have to work for the salvation of the soul from the captivity of the body. Unfortunately, this notion of human body looms large in the Christian understanding of body. We have clear negation of this in the John's Gospel and also in the writings of Paul. In a context in which matter was considered as evil, John says: "*The Word became flesh and dwelt among us*" (Jn. 1:14). Paul also emphasizes that the human body is the temple of God and the bodily functions should be in proximity to the Spirit of God.

What is dominant in the distorted Greek notions is the dualistic tendencies of the ancient Greek vis-à-vis Gnostic philosophy. Dualistic tendencies such as body–soul, this world–other world, sacred–profane, divine–secular were prevalent in the early church due to the onslaught of the Greek mindset. This even resulted in the negative attitudes to human body by considering it as the seat of all evil. Some even made a dichotomy between the bodily actions and actions of the spirit.

b. Hebrew View of Body

It has been pointed out by Biblical scholars that the Hebrews didn't have a separate word for *body*. The nearest equivalent for body in Hebrew is *basar* which can be translated as *flesh* which is considered as an inclusive term for the whole body; it refers to the whole person. There is no dichotomy between the body and soul in Hebrew thinking. Similarly, the Hebrews didn't make a sharp distinction between the body and soul. This is the theological basis for the resurrection of the body in Christian faith. The Hebrew equivalent for soul is *nephesh*, which occurs in the Hebrew Bible, means soul, self, person, life, living being, etc. In other words, *basar* (flesh) is not just a part of man, but the whole man considered in his weakness and corruptibility, physical, and moral...The body is the outwardness of the soul and the soul is the inwardness of the body.[2]

Biblical scholars also point out that the *nephesh* (soul) is closely related to *ruah* (spirit), the life giving principle and energy (Gen.1). As opposed to the

Greek and Gnostic traditions, the Hebrew thought emphasizes the unitive and holistic function of human body. Similarly, the Hebrews did not make a contrast between the whole body and its parts. In other words, here each part of the body represents the whole person. Paul uses this metaphor of the body in his doctrine of the church in 1 Corinthians 11. What we have here is the spiritual significance of human body.

c. Market View of Human Body

As pointed out earlier, in the contemporary Global market, human body is only a commodity. Several of the market products are for beautification, such as colour, fragrance, and wellness of the body. Very often the white body is glorified over against the black body. Thanks to the Black Liberation movement, the search for black identity and black consciousness, which affirmed unequivocally, Black is beautiful (Song of Solomon 1:5). S. Kappen writes powerfully: *In the capitalist society, body is reduced to an item of private property, into an instrument of competition and aggression.*[3] It is as if, there is no salvation outside the market ideology! In one of his lectures in Bangalore on Globalization, he said, "*A pseudo-Trinity is at work in our world: Market, Materialism and, Media.*" These three are very often considered as the pillars of Globalization. In this system, body is a consumer product, a sex-object, a medium of exploitation. What is at stake here is the reverence for body and its functions in the community. Hence, a contemporary version of the Pauline concern would be the redemption of the body from its market wrappings! Unfortunately, this reductionist approach of the body is not taken seriously in our concept of salvation, which is dominated by the Greek thinking even today that salvation is of the soul alone. Here we are losing sight of the Hebrew notion of body which emphasizes the sacredness of the body and its functions.

d. The Objectified Body

There are several historical examples of the objectification and mutilation of the human body in many countries. Here are two examples from the United States and India. In the US the blacks were subjected to severe punishments during the period of white racist supremacy. The enslaved Africans (now Afro-Americans or blacks), could be sold, purchased, and mutilated. Their captive body was no longer subject but object. Moreover, as object the body is not so much the representation of *otherness* but, in physical and biological expression and in response to it, becomes an *other thing*. Thus slavery objectified the black body as an object of property, an object of production.[4] On the whole, the system of slavery, which was approved by the law in those days, sought to deprive the blacks of their personhood and identity. Thanks to the Black Liberation Movement under the leadership of Martin Luther King Jr and several others, this system has been significantly, even if not totally, overturned. If this was several decades ago in US, we have a similar situation in the world's biggest democratic country, India.

In several of the North Indian States, especially in Utter Pradesh, mob lynching is a reality. Here the victims are mostly the Dalits and the poor Muslims, who are mostly in the meat industry. In a study on mob lynching by the Centre for the Study of Society and Secularism in Mumbai, Irfan Engineer, a noted sociologist and a few others have brought to the fore the heart wrenching issues of mob lynching over incidents such as cow slaughter, consumption of beef, etc. The report says that in spite of the intervention of the Supreme Court of India, this dehumanizing menace has increased under the leadership of the right wing Hindutva groups. The report concludes as follows:

> *Though the political landscape of India is fast changing with discriminating legislations and resistance, mob lynching has been a reality to deal with. This reality doesn't just haunt and scar the survivors of mob lynching and their families but also the moral conscience of India. Or at least one expects it should have.*[5]

In the world over, even in our post-modern times, women's body is considered as an object of sex, as a commodity! Feminists continuously declare to the male chauvinists in all religious traditions that their body is their inherent right and is to be respected. In some of the recent mob lynching issues in North India, the bodies of Dalits and Muslims were objectified and mutilated. This was mainly on the accusations that they either ate beef or traded beef. Several of the NGO's revealed that the culprits are mainly the *go-rakshas* (cow vigilantes) in the North. This was mainly in the State of Upper Pradesh.

These are definitely expressions of the objectification and mutilation of human body, where the victims are the less privileged and powerless and very often their voices fall on the deaf ears of the ruling class. These are all inhuman, sacrilegious, and idolatrous practices which not only violate the integrity and sacredness of human body; it is also blaspheme against the incarnate body of Jesus Christ.

e. Christian View of Body

A question that is very often asked in Christian anthropology is whether the body has a defining role in human existence. Is the human body intrinsically good or evil?

The body is always with us; it is inseparable from us. It is the mediator of our engagement with the world. But, the body is no mere object with which we are confronted; the body is something that we ourselves are.[6] For example, the human bodily needs such as hunger, thirst, pleasure, pain, or desire for acceptance, search for values, self-determination – all these are part of human body and hence human being. In other words, what we need to underscore is the unitive function of human body which is both psychological as well as theological. It is simple logic that life is more than eating, drinking, enjoying, and amassing wealth. We know that some are sex enthusiasts, some are journey enthusiasts, some are pleasure enthusiasts, and some are wealth enthusiasts and so on. But the pivotal question is h*ow does the human body embody and manifest the human person*?

Boff writes, "*In the Bible, body is the entire human being – and preciously as person, communicating in, communicating itself to, and forming the network of vital relationship with surrounding reality. Body, then, is synonymous with person.*"[7]

Paul confronts this issue in his letters. For example, in Romans 12:1-2 "*So, then my brothers, because of God's mercy to us, I appeal to you: offer your bodies as a living sacrifice to God, dedicated to his service and pleasing to him.*" In 1 Corinthians 6:19-20, he highlights the spiritual significance of human body. In an age of co-modification of human body, this is a valuable insight. The Christian Gnostics in the early centuries taught that human bodily actions won't affect the soul provided proper prayers are said. This led to immorality in the churches, especially in Corinth. Here they failed to understand that in all human actions, human body is involved. According to Paul, the church is the 'Body of Christ.' It is one body with many parts.

> "*Christ is like a single body, which has many parts; it is still one body, even though it is made up of many parts. In the same way, all of us, whether Jews or Gentiles, whether slaves or free, have been baptized into the one body by the same Spirit, and we have all been given the one Spirit to drink*" (1 Cor12:12).

Christian Church history tells us that this metaphor of the church as the 'Body of Christ' was a powerful weapon in the fight against several of the social evils like apartheid in South Africa and casteism in India, etc. The body metaphor also points out that the body of Christ is the wounded body and the broken body and so the church ought to manifest such a lifestyle in its historical actions and options.

In the early stages of Maramon convention in the 1880's, which is billed as the biggest Christian gathering in Asia, the Syrians and Dalits didn't have social fellowship. Even sitting together under a common roof and listening to the word was considered as a revolutionary step! In such a context, Mandapathil Achen, (Achen in Malayalam means clergy) and a few others organized fellowship meals after the sessions to emphasize the body metaphor of the church. This action in those days faced stiff opposition from the caste-ridden Syrian Christians! Poikayil Yohannan, a Dalit evangelist had to leave the Mar Thoma church, having challenged its so-called Syrian ethnicity. Well, the official version of the church is that the word 'Syrian' along with its name is neither clannish nor ethnic but liturgical. But the question is whether the church can truly become the 'Body of Christ' as we very often claim.

2. Productive Ageing

In a Senior citizen's forum meeting, the person who welcomed the gathering said "I am now 75 years young!" This attitude is common among the elderly. We always want to romanticize the young age. A joke is there in Kerala about a politician who in his 90's asks his cook who was only in his 30's, "Who is there to cook for me after your death?" Surprisingly in many places, especially in the West, efforts are under way in the field of research in the area of ageing and also costly surgeries to remove your wrinkles from skin and so on! But this is only an attempt to do away with the reality of ageing which is part of God's plan.

A long life is usually the desire of anyone who is in a well-knit family; with sufficient care and protection of body, mind and spirit. Some may become worn out by old age and start counting down as they advance in years! Thus old age can be understood in different ways: as a path of decline towards the inevitable death or as a path of progress towards the fullness of life.

Is long life a blessing? In the Old Testament, it is promised to those who honour the Lord (Ex 20:12). In the Wisdom Literature, it is pictured as a crown for the one who is just, and also he has the joy of seeing his children's children (Prov. 10:27, 17:6). In almost all cultures of the world, there is a special reverence to those who are old. In the Hindu tradition, there is a practice that blessings are sought from the senior most in the family prior to marriage and other occasions like a significant assessment test and so on. In the Jewish tradition and Christian traditions, we have similar practices: "*You shall stand up before the grey head, and honour the face of an old man, and you shall fear your God; I am the Lord*" (Lev. 19:32).

a. Problems of Seniors

The problems of seniors are manifold, such as health hazards, economic depravity, feeling of rejection in families and in the community, anxiety, and so on. Even in the context of COVID 19, they are at a higher risk, according to those in the medical field. This is mainly due to their decreased immunity and bodily reserves as well as the associated health hazards like diabetes, hypertension, etc. Above all, physical immobility becomes an important handicap to those who are mentally and intellectually alert.

The transition in the Kerala society from joint family to nuclear family, and from agrarian culture to industrial culture, made the life of the seniors more pathetic. Though the care of the elderly is considered as a virtue in the Indian culture; since most of the children are working abroad, the parents and grandparents are either left to the maids or some are in assisted home facilities. I remember having visited a senior person who was perhaps, over eighty-years old and almost confined to bed. Six of his children were working abroad and all well settled. He was under the care of an assistant. With tears in his eyes, he said, "Achen, I wish I had one among my children; perhaps not too educated, to take care of me at this age!" This could be construed as a negative and selfish approach; but it should be seen as the plight of the seniors in our context.

Well, solutions are not that easy. One of them is nursing homes or day care centres. This has already become the practice in the West. Whereas in the Kerala context, due to sociological reasons and also due to the concept of family system, this is yet to be taken as a viable practice.

b. Self-identity of the Seniors

Two areas are to be recognized here. First, how do the seniors look upon themselves and secondly, how do others look at them? In some places the self-sufficiency of the seniors creates problems. They won't let anyone do anything. I am reminded of one of my Parishes, where the Sunday school teachers were mostly old people. In those days in the Mar Thoma Church there was no upper age limit for the Sunday school teachers (now it is 70). Finally, in the general Body meeting of the Sunday school teachers, I suggested that a graceful retirement should be given to our teachers who have crossed 70. A programme was fixed, and people were asked to relinquish their post. Surprisingly, it worked and a new team of teachers was selected!

While giving due recognition to our seniors, and respecting their wisdom, there is also a danger to be noted in the self-identity of the seniors: they can be very assertive and unwilling to make any changes in the way they think and act. This kind of self-sufficiency of the seniors very often creates chaotic situations in the family and community. A story is told about a flight engineer. After his training, prior to the first trial trip in the sky, he went home for a few days. He was directed by his parents to receive the blessings and advise from the grandfather, who was in his 90's. He blessed the grandson and also gave this advice: Do not take too much speed and do not fly too high as it would be dangerous! The grandfather's ignorance of the aerodynamics is understandable; but the point is that in our old age we should not insist that we have our say on everything; let it be in the family or church. This happens to some of our church and political leaders who are tempted to think that after them it will be a deluge! Reminiscences are good provided others are ready to listen; otherwise it would be a self-glorification of the past.

In several of the families in Kerala, only a few old parents would on their own arrange the partition of the properties and assets gracefully. In some places, this leads to family conflicts, sibling rivalry and even court cases.

How do our families approach the seniors? Are they seen as a liability, an old stock to be evacuated anytime? The basic question is whether we can we create a family environment which provides space for all?

c. Graceful Ageing

I remember this as the theme of the Kuttapuzha Parish where I served several years ago. Each meeting was set apart for one particular dimension of the theme. For example, the medical, psychological, Biblical were some of the sub-themes.

It is to be acknowledged that within the churches we have started senior citizen fellowships, regular visits of those who confined to homes, palliative care schemes and so on. But, we are yet to chalk out an effective support system for the senior members. I am reminded of one Parish in North India where they have a help line facility for the members who are needy. I also recall the comments made by a medical doctor in a senior citizen's fellowship, "Now it seems more importance should be given to geriatrics than paediatrics." It is very often pointed out that geriatrics is not a major area of study and research in India as it is in the medical colleges in the West.

A few Biblical insights are helpful here. "*Do not cast me off in the time of old age; forsake me not when my strength is spent*" (Ps. 71:9) "*They still bear fruit in old age; they are ever full of sap and green, to declare that the Lord is upright; he is my rock and there is no unrighteousness in him*" (Ps. 92:14,15). Here 'bearing fruit in old age' is not to be seen as the ability to work in old age as was in the youth or middle age. Rather, this is the God-given ability to be serene, to be compassionate, and composed.

Here the Psalmist recognizes the reality of ageing; what he needs is the providential care of God so that he will fulfil his mission in life. In the East, there is an emphasis to the "Power of silence." According to the Patristic fathers, the climax of speech is silence. Perhaps, old age is a time to recapture this vision; a time to recapitulate, review, and rediscover our inner spiritual potentials.

Very often it is said that two categories of people would find their old age too difficult: teachers and clergy. Both of them, in a way are value producers and they always would like to make others listen to them; but seldom do they listen! As someone has rightly commented, the best way to make others listen to you is to make yourself worth listening. So instead of creating voice pollution, let us learn to be silent and develop the skills of listening.

Well, the concern of this section was not so much to go in to the sociological dimensions of the senior citizens; but rather, the effort was mainly to bring out some of the vital issues and how to address them so that the church would be a facilitator of hope in the community.

3. Theology of Death

Death is an inevitable reality of life on earth. Very often people are hesitant to reflect on death, because of the thinking that it may spoil one's pleasure in living. All medical interventions are either to overcome death or to postpone it. Different religions in the world have made different attempts to define death; to grapple with the meaning of death.

A few of the Patristic thinkers were of the view that God invented death as a kind of remedy for sin. "Without death sin is in danger of becoming immortal; whereas with death, sin can be removed once and for all."[8] The question here is this: Does human sin deface or efface the *imago Dei*? The New Testament witness is that Jesus confronted the forces of sin at the personal and social level; nevertheless, he does not give anyone the capacity to do away with sin or the power not to commit sin. It does not mean that sin is inevitable in human life; rather it points to human propensity to sin and also its historical ambiguities.

Samuel Rayan challenges us to view death in a positive way as follows:

One: It is the act in which a person finally gathers himself up, brings all his life into focus, and gives himself a definitive structure...an act in which one completes himself...

Two: It is an event through which one acquires an all cosmic relationship... Death is therefore a new way of being ourselves.

Three: It is dying to rise to an all cosmic-relationship; struggling to get beyond our divisive and death dealing structures of caste and class, and create a free society without domination and manipulation.[9]

While acknowledging the fact that we cannot rationalize everything due to our finitude; some observations are necessary:

- Can we say that all sufferings and deaths are God's will?
- Is there space for human will within God's will?
- Is God's will subject to change?
- Don't we need to make a distinction between death due to old age and that of children's or youth's death?

I have confronted several such issues in my pastoral ministry so far. The simple or perhaps, the simplistic answer of the clergy goes like this: When somebody is born into this world, God sets a life span. He decides when a person should die and that too, how! Another explanation is that, God loves you so much so that he needs you in heaven! There are fancy stories here, such as the children will become bright stars in heaven, they will be appointed for various tasks in heaven and so on. I am reminded of one of the burial services in Bangalore in the 90's. Since I was doing my doctoral study at that time; I didn't have the responsibility of a parish. This was the burial of a school boy, who died in a school bus accident. The Vicar asked me to give a brief message during the service. I had difficulty in saying that the death of that boy was God's will. This was mainly because of two reasons: One, the driver of the bus was known for his reckless driving. Two, the School Management did not take proper action against the driver even after receiving several complaints from the parents of the children. Well, when we say that the death is God's will, it may serve as a word of temporal consolation for the family. But, are we not either justifying the action or inaction of the School Management and the bus driver? What we need is a more realistic approach.

We have the unfolding of the Old Testament theology of the suffering and death of the righteous in the Wisdom tradition, especially in the book of Job. In the book we find Job challenging the traditional Jewish theology, expounded and defended by his friends, that suffering is due to sin. The Psalmist struggles with the same question:

> Therefore the people turn and praise them, and find no fault in them.
> And they say, "How can God know? Is there knowledge in the Most High?"
> Such are the wicked; always at ease, they increase in riches.
> All in vain I have kept my heart clean and washed my hands in innocence.
> For all day long I have been plagued, and am punished every morning...
> Truly you set them in slippery places; you make them fall to ruin.
> How they are destroyed in a moment, swept away utterly by terrors!
> *Nevertheless, I am continuously with you; you hold my right hand* (Ps. 73:10-14, 18-19, 23).

In both cases, rather than metaphysical arguments, the emphasis is on a profound experience of the divine presence. Here suffering becomes a mystery and also a revelation of the divine. We cannot comprehend it; but we can go beyond it in our journey of faith. Yes, what matters in the context of suffering and bereavement are the all-embracing presence of the Divine and our presence with the afflicted without making any fatalistic, deterministic, or value judgmental comments! Paul gives the assurance that with the power of the risen Christ, we have victory over the powers of sin (1Cor.15:57).

It is said that King Philip, the father of Alexander the Great (359-336 BC) had an official in his palace and his duty was to say to the King every morning: Philip, you will die! Here death is considered simply as a reminder of one's finitude in life, his or her mortal nature. Death can also be understood in a different way: that a meaningful life is a prerequisite to a meaningful death. In an in-depth article on the "*Let Us Learn to Die*" in Malayalam, George Behanan, a counsellor and therapist brings this out. According to him, the thought of death would make some active and energetic, whereas others become frightened. He also cites an example from the Titanic tragedy. The huge Titanic ship sank on April 15, 1912. Ensuring the swift rescue operation, the Captain of the ship took note of one lady, who was given three minutes to collect her essentials. She ran to her room and came back with three oranges. Yes, at the point of death, there is always a reversal of values![10] Recently, this has happened in the context of the nationwide lockdown in India. People did not go for cars, smart phones, or new houses but all were running for milk, provisions, vegetables, etc.

As a Clergy, I have witnessed a few people dying; or perhaps, the way they responded in the context of an impending death. The one that I cherish most is the last times of Rev. Dr. M. A. Thomas, the founder of the Ecumenical Christian Centre, Bangalore. On his request, he was given Unction (considered as one of the sacraments in the Eastern tradition). I was there for the service which was officiated by the Diocesan Bishop, Bishop Theodosius at the Bangalore East Mar Thoma Church. Thomas Achen, though physically weak, was serene throughout the service. After the service, I had an opportunity to assist him to get into his car. As he was about to leave; he turned to Bishop Theodosius and asked in a feeble voice, "Thirumeni, what is your programme in the evening; are you in the city this evening, say, after 5 pm? Thirumeni said: Yes Achen, I am here and free in the evening." If my memory is correct, Achen died around 5.30 pm! In the memorial service some one said: M. A. Thomas Achen was a good planner; he even planned his own death! This is not to say that you can predict the time of your death; but rather, if you have lived a fuller life, you can face death cheerfully.

Some consider it as an inevitable human destiny, non-existence of being, sleep, etc. and it is beyond the scope of this section to go into those details.

In Jewish faith, the "dead are no more", they "are gone for ever" (Ps. 39:13; Job 7:8,21). Jews considered the state of the dead as a "state of silence" (Ps. 115:17). According to Psalm 88, the Lord himself forgets the dead. (Vs. 6,7)! It was the common Jewish belief that from the state of Sheol, there is no return whatsoever (Job 10:21ff). Perhaps, the only Old Testament portion which gives a different view is Daniel 12:2. Here we have more hope for the dead and they are not gone for ever.

In all cultures, the dead bodies are given respect and proper burial. In Judaism and Christian faith, the dead are buried and in Hinduism, there is the practice of cremation which is considered as more eco-friendly in nature. In the Mar Thoma liturgy for burial, the term 'farewell' is used which has an element of hope. The approach to those who commit suicide has always been a problem in the different church traditions. Several of the churches will not give a Christian burial to those who commit suicide. This 'moralistic approach' was challenged through a private resolution in the Mar Thoma Sabha Mandalam in the 90's (the supreme decision-making body in the church). Dr. A. J. John who moved the resolution, had a two-fold argument: One – No normal human will commit suicide. If somebody commits suicide; perhaps due to poverty or depression, that person alone cannot be held responsible for such a decision. Two – The burial service in the Mar Thoma church is for the peace and consolation of the bereaved family and not for the departed soul. If so, the church has an obligation to such families. Though the resolution met stiff opposition from one section in the church, who were of the view that no one has the right to take way his/her life, or the practice would increase the number of suicides in the church and so on; finally it was approved. I remember having supported the resolution. Afterwards, a special liturgy was created and now the clergy can give Christian burial to those who commit suicide. This is not to glorify the practice of suicides. Here we have a duty to ask the question: Why some people commit suicide? Reasons may be many, such as depression, feelings of rejection, failure in examinations, broken heartedness, etc. Instead of penalizing the bereaved family, the question is whether we can become a grace-filled community in which graceful deaths are possible.

Jesus enables us to accept death as a reality. He also challenges us to face death gracefully. His conversation with Martha and Mary in the context of the death of Lazarus makes it clear. He says: "*I am the resurrection and life; whoever believes in me will live, even though he dies, and whoever lives and believes in me will never die*" (Jn. 11:24-25). This text is popularly seen as the one which narrates the story of Lazarus who was brought to life. But the question is whether it has to do with an extension of life to Lazarus. I would say that the focus is on the enduring truth that Jesus proclaims in the context of death: "*I am the resurrection and life.*" Such an approach would enable us to face death meaningfully and with hope.

As pointed out earlier, as a Clergy, I have conducted numerous burial services; those of young and old. Irrespective of the age, I have seen people dying in peace and harmony. The fact is that in spite of the Christian belief in heaven and eternity, all of us would like to live life to the fullest. Some would like to see the marriages of their children; some others would like to see their grandchildren, even some others look forward to their great grandchildren! Yes, though the passion for life is good; let us also accept the reality that life has an end. Hence, what matters is our preparedness to die. In the counselling classes in the Seminary, students are taught how to prepare church members for a graceful death. But only few Clergy would take those lessons seriously or try to develop on them in the light of their pastoral situations and challenges. In the light of my own pastoral experience for the last several decades, on a few occasions could I see church members dying in peace and contentment. In the Mar Thoma Church, there is a liturgy for the sacrament of Unction.[11] Even if the Vicar asks someone who is nearing death whether he would like to have Communion, or Unction, the family would be hesitant! It doesn't mean that such a Communion is inevitable, or it would ensure one's entry into heaven. This is just to say how unprepared we are within the church to face death. Paul talks about the state of the dead in 1 Corinthians.

> *For what is mortal must be changed into what is immortal; what will die must be changed into what cannot die. So when this takes place and the mortal has been changed into the immortal, then the scripture will come true. Death is destroyed; victory is complete! Where death is your victory? Where Death is your power to hurt? Death gets its power to hurt from sin, and sin gets its power from the Law. But thanks be to God who gives us the victory through our Lord, Jesus Christ!* (1Cor. 15:51-56).

Paul considers death as the final enemy who was conquered by Jesus through his resurrection. There is a notion in Christian circles that death came to this world due to the sin of Adam and Eve and Jesus Christ confronted death. But, even if Adam had not sinned, there would have been physical death. For example, even after their disobedience, they didn't die, as the serpent promised them! (Gen 3:4). Hence, what Jesus confronts is not the experience or reality of death but the fear of death. This was the faith of several of the faithful in history who faced death cheerfully in the context of persecution.

4. Resurrection of the Body or Immortality of the Soul?

While the 'Immortality of the soul' is found in Greek and Hindu religious traditions, the Christian concept is the 'Resurrection of the Body.' Paul makes is clear in 1 Corinthians. The problem with the concept of the immortality of the soul is that it is totally impersonal. This is to be understood in the context of the Greek and Indian god concepts which are mostly impersonal in nature. This is the emphasis in *Advaita* (Monism) philosophy developed by Sankara in India; where as in *VishIsta Advaita* (Qualified Monism) of Ramanuja and a few others, we have the personal dimension of God. The concept of resurrection challenges the spiritualism of Plato and the materialism of Aristotle. Two issues in the concept of the immortality of the soul are that the soul is imperishable, both in Greek and Hindu traditions; and that the concept of the soul that is alienated from the body.

Paul reminds us:

> *Someone will ask: How can the dead be raised to life? What kind of body will they have? You fool! When you saw a seed in the ground, it does not sprout to life unless it dies. And what you saw is a bare seed, perhaps a grain of wheat or some other grain, not the full-bodied plant that will later grow up. God provides that seed with the body he wishes; he gives each seed its own proper body* (1Cor 15:35-38).

In other words, the resurrection, as N. T. Wright states, is "a way of talking about a new bodily life after whatever state of existence one might enter immediately upon death. It was, in other words, life after life after death."[12] Here the focus is that the resurrected body is a transformed body. The basis of this transformation is the death and resurrection of Christ.

This has been an area of debate in Christian theology. The question can be summarized like this: Did faith cause resurrection or did resurrection cause faith? As pointed out earlier, the crucifixion of Jesus was an objective historical event; but the resurrection was a subjective experience of the disciples and the early church. Both are to be seen within the perspective of Christian faith.

The way of life is through death as evidenced in Jesus' response to the Greek seekers:

> *I am telling you the truth: a grain of wheat remains no more than a single grain unless it is dropped into the ground and dies. If it does die, then it produces many grains. Whoever loves his own life will lose it; whoever hates his own life in this world will keep it for life eternal"* (Jn 12:22-25).

Here Jesus is challenging the Greek concept of God that He is beyond sufferings and underscoring the way of life through death, which is the way of the Cross. This kenotic dimension of life is at the core of the Christian theology of death. In other words, there is no rising without a passion, without the way of the cross.

5. Victory Over the Powers of Death

Paul's words in I Corinthians are clear. "O death where is your victory? Your power to hurt? Death gets it power to hurt from sin; and sin gets its power from the Law. But thanks be to God who gives us the victory through our Lord, Jesus Christ!" (1 Cor. 15:55-56).

The power of resurrection is not limited to the Christian Church; it pervades the whole cosmos. This power enables us to go beyond in all spheres of life. Here both the existential and the eschatological dimensions of faith are heavily interwoven. The power of resurrection is not the power to rule over others, to domesticate, to make exclusive truth claims, or to take revenge on those who crucified Jesus; but it is the power to redeem, the power to transform, the power to initiate discipleship and mission, the power to be with the forces of life in the world.

The risen Christ challenges us with new questions in our areas of defeat and professional excellence. He confronted Simon Peter and other disciples in their despair and challenges them to 'throw their net into the deep waters' (Lk. 5:4; Jn. 21:6). What we need in any attempt to transform the local spaces is the willingness to throw our net into the deep waters, i.e., the attempt to go beyond the superficial ideological assumptions to the deeper realities of life. This will eventually enable us to rejoice with the risen Christ with what we have caught afresh (Jn. 21:10).

Ageing is not to be seen as a disease; it is part of God's plan for us. Death is to be accepted as a reality and not as a tragedy. All of us would like to have a full life; say eighty or more. But the aspect of our mortality should not be ignored. What we have contributed to the world is more important than how long we live. Our hope is not that we will go to heaven after this life; but that this life lived in relationship with God and others is not in vain and we are not sure as to what is in store for us. Instead of making heaven as a place to go at the end, let us create a heavenly atmosphere wherever we are; that is a life with God and God's concern for this world.

15

Church as a Community of Hope

Christian Hope is not a facile optimism or a wishful thinking. Rather, it's a resistance movement with God against all forces of sin and evil; all fatalistic and deterministic tendencies, in all fields-religious, cultural, political economic and so on. What we need as a community of faith is a realistic introspection into ourselves; whether are vindicating the claims we make for ourselves, as a community of hope. Do we really facilitate hope amidst hopelessness or despair or are we stumbling blocks in the way of hope? Our task is to discern and promote signs of hope around us; within us, perhaps as search for alternatives or as 'little narratives or protest voices and traditions', within the church and outside the church.

Community is to be understood as a web of human relationships and not a collection of individuals. The Christian church is basically a community of faith, a community of communities. The search for a community of faith should always be within the framework of the wider human community. The basic search here is for the dignity and self-identity of human communities cutting across religious, caste, linguistic, and communal affiliations. In spite of all forces of death and anti-life; there are elements of hope in several fields such as art, literature, science, politics, and so on. In Greek philosophy, hope is a neutral expectation, a wishful thinking which can be either pleasant or unpleasant. It has different aspects such as, illusory acceptance, rational prospect, existential confidence, etc. In Plato, it is reaching out of the soul to the future in a transcendent way.

1. Christian Community within the Human Community

Here the role of the church is to be understood as a community of faith within the wider community. Our parishes are not to be narrow, communal, ethnic, and parochial entities. The Bangkok Assembly of EACC in 1964 rightly chose as its theme "The Christian Community within the Wider Human Community." The document of the Assembly challenged the Asian Christians to become aware of the meaning and implication of the Christian presence in the situations and occupations in which they and their fellow men are placed by God. The challenge here is to do away with the narrow and parochial loyalties. Here it should be remembered that any unity at local levels should not be the cause of disunity at higher levels. For instance, many of our narrow linguistic and ethnic communities such as Hindutva and Khalistan in India or perhaps, the Jewish and Christian Zionist movements in the West, very often threaten the very fabric of the wider community in our times. Instead of homogenization of culture and language, what we need today is the recognition and promotion of diversity within our social milieu. No culture is static in nature. What is to be underscored is the interpenetration of cultures in our search for the wider human community. In several of Tagore's poems we have this element of hope:

> *I will keep still and wait like the night.*
> *With its starry vigil and its head bent low with patience.*
> *The morning will surely come,*
> *The darkness will vanish, and thy voice pour down.*
> *In golden streams breaking through the sky,*
> *Then thy words will take wing in songs...*
> *And thy melodies will break forth in flowers,*
> *In all my forest groves* (Githanjali).

The main theme of the 8th Assembly of WCC, which was held in Harare, Zimbabwe in 1998 was "Turn to God and Rejoice in Hope." Ecumenical Christian Centre, Bangalore conducted a Consultation on this theme and the papers are published in the *Theology for Our Times*, May 1996. In his position paper on the theme, Mathai Zacharia points out that we should not find easy security when faced with the pressures and demonic forces around us. He also suggests that we make our hope an ethical action.

> "*The sense of the present possession, to have and not to wait – this is the opposite of hope. To rejoice in hope means to know God in hope without seeing Him, and to be satisfied that it should be so. This is what makes hope an ethical action; for to hope in God turns hope into an ethical act which cannot be brought to naught.*"[1]

In other words, Christian hope is not merely an attitude, a wishful thinking that in the end everything will be all right with God's help. Rather, it is a hope in action which continuously reminds us that whatever happens, in our lives and around us, nothing can prevent us from fulfilling the ultimate meaning of our existence.

2. Making a Difference in God's Way

Abraham was called by God to be the founder of a new community; a community that is set apart for God's purpose in history. But the calling narrative in Gen 12:1-4 is very often understood in the light of the doctrine of Election which is always associated with nationalistic pride, privileges, authority, ethnic and patriarchal hegemony. The development of the theme is found in Deuteronomy 7:6-11. Genesis 17:5-6 affirms that God will make nations of Abraham. Abraham was not called the father of an ethnic group or nation or religion. The culmination of the theme is found in the 'Suffering Servant songs' in Isaiah. Through Abraham, the community of Israel was chosen as God's alternative community and suffering servant in history. The basic nature of God as revealed in the call Abraham is a world-oriented God who wants human beings as his partners on earth. Here the call is to be with God and God's purposes in the world. It should be noticed here that God's agenda is the world and not merely the community of Israel or the church. In the call of Abraham, we also find a radical departure from polytheism to monotheism.

Paul writes to in Romans:

> *Through Him we have obtained the access to the grace in which we stand, and we rejoice in our hope of sharing the glory of God. Not only that, but we rejoice in our sufferings knowing that suffering produces endurance, and endurance produces character, and character produces hope, and hope does not put us to shame, because God's love has been poured into our hearts through the Holy Spirit who has been given to us* (Rom. 5:2-5).

Again, in the twelfth chapter ,he writes:"*Rejoice in your hope, be patient in tribulation, be constant in prayer*" (Rom 12:12).

This is hope in the midst of despair, in the context of hopelessness. Here our call is also to march toward an unknown future in hope. The call is not to make one's life safe and secure but to make it authentic and worth living. This is basically a vocation which has to do with the sacredness of life; a vision-oriented life, a purpose-driven life. Here faith becomes a journey into the uncertainties of life with God. According to C. S. Song, "*Faith is the power to see the vision of tomorrow in the darkness of today...Faith is the living power that enables us to maintain our sanity in this maddening world of threats, torture, and solitary confinement. Faith is the energy that makes it possible for us to maintain the balance of the spirit in this age of change and insecurity. Faith is the grace given to you by God, enabling you to reach out for life when confronted with death.*"[2]

3. The Wider Family of God

As mentioned above, the call of Abraham was a call to be the harbinger of God's wider family. What does it mean when God says, "Leave your native land, your kindred and your father's house; and go to a country that I am going to show you."

(Gen 12:1). God wants Abraham to begin a journey of faith and hope. This also means the basic preparedness to have a new set of values, lifestyle, culture, and so on. What is of great importance is to transcend one's narrow family framework, mindset, and values in order to be within the wider family of God. This is for new priorities in life. The call is not necessarily from one place to another but from one state of life to another; from what we are to what we ought to be. God wants all of us to be with him on earth.

St. Paul presents God as the absolute home maker; the one who is always in the process of creating his wider family on earth. The ultimate purpose of God revealed to us in the person and work of Christ is that the entire creation and the whole humanity will be fully united into the one family of God (Eph 1:9-10). In this wider family of God all the man made 'walls of partition' are transcended (Col 3:11; Gal 3:28). Reconciliation is God's initiative in Christ (1 Cor 5:17-18). The emergence of the new always involves pain, struggles, and suffering. Romans 8:19-26 talks about the three-fold groaning for the new birth within the universal family of God namely the sub-human creation, humanity, and the divine Spirit. The church of Christ is called to articulate this three-fold groaning of nature, humanity and God and to work with the Spirit as mid-wife to make the birth happen–fragmentarily now and fully at the end.

4. Faith Response to Crisis Situations of Life

Let me make an attempt to do an evaluation of three recent events: The Tsunami, the Delhi riots, and the COVID 19. The first is a natural catastrophe, the second a human made violence and its aftermath, and the third is a pandemic. In the Tsunami, several thousands lost their lives and livestock. The worst affected places were Indonesia, Sri Lanka, and India. The recent Delhi riots were in the context of peoples' response to the new Citizens' Amendment Bill of the Government of India. The worst affected people are the Muslims, especially the poor ones. It was reported on media that in some places in Delhi, the culprits even asked for the religion of the people at their doorsteps before setting the houses ablaze. The causalities due to the COVID pandemic are in the millions, and the worst affected places are China, Italy, USA and India. In the first phase of the COVID prevention, the efforts of the Kerala Health Department were commendable. These involve home quarantine, community kitchens, isolation departments in hospitals etc. Food and medicines are supplied to them for free! In spite of all these efforts, presently the situation is alarming, mainly due to community spread. The swift and complete lock down declared by the central Government, though on the advice that social distance is one of the ways to contain the virus; has left the lives of several lakhs of migrant workers and daily wage earners to penury and marginalization. Hence, according to media reports, several of them had to return home breaking the lock down protocol. Several of them say that if they continue where they are without work, they will die of hunger; if they return home, even if they die of COVID, they can die with their families! What a tragic situation. Now, let me bring out five responses to the issues mentioned above.

One: The agnostic, atheist response

This leisure time kind of response is mainly in the social media. Some have come forward and asked: "Where is your God? What is the validity of religion and rituals? How dare you cancel your worship services and other rituals? Don't you think at least now that only science has the solutions to these kind of issues." Well, the question here is whether this is a creation of our science and technology, especially in the field of biological weapons. And the U.S and China are blaming each other as to who is primarily responsible. I am not trying to make any value judgments here. As pointed out earlier, several of the ministers in the Left Front ruling Government are either agnostics or atheists. Nevertheless, they are not trying to prove or disprove anything here. They are busy working for the people such as vigilant preventive measures, awareness programmes, support systems at different levels, etc.

Two: The Market/Corporate response

They are worried that the markets and their profits are going down. A person in Calicut was taken into custody by the police for hoarding masks and sanitizers! Notwithstanding the fact that the COVID crisis is also an economic crisis; the basic question is who are the worst affected people and what are the measures that are under way to sustain them. The huge exodus of migrant workers to their homeland is an aftermath of the crisis. Besides the present arrangement of the Indian Railways to transport them to their homelands, their plight is yet to be resolved in a country like India.

Three: The Biblical literalists' response

As usual, for them these are all signs of the end! There is nothing that can be done in this context, except prayer and fasting so that the Lord would do something. As pointed out earlier in the section on Biblical hermeneutics, this is an evasive and unchristian kind of response.

Four: The moralistic response

There are media reports about kind of a moral policing in the State of Maharashtra. There, surprisingly, the suspected COVID patients are given some kind of a mark in their bodies. The Government's logic is that it is for the community health. Nevertheless, the fact is that they are stigmatized in the community; and in some places they find it difficult to travel for their essential needs; not even to the hospitals! In Kerala, the most literate state in India, there are reports about people blocking the burial of COVID patients as they fear that would transmit the disease in the neighbourhood of the cemetery!

Five: The Kingdom response

For example, I am reminded of an inter-religious prayer, a Remembrance Day in the context of Tsunami in New York in which a special collection was taken for the relief work in Indonesia. This amount plus the collections from the churches were sent for relief work through the National Council of Churches in USA. I was on the Executive Board of the NCC-USA, especially on the Justice and Peace Commission during this period, representing the Diocese of North America and Europe of the Mar Thoma Church. In the context of the Delhi riots, the National Council of Churches in India (NCCI) initiated an inter–religious prayer and they visited the families of the victims. Several churches offered their buildings as refugee centres. In Kerala, now church youth groups are engaged in the distribution of food and medicines to those who are in isolation camps. Well, what we need in situations such as this is not abstract philosophical or theological responses but concrete and passionate actions. Let us remind ourselves that the presence of God is to be sought in our response to tragedies and not necessarily within the tragedies. Along with that, we have the do away with the usual disciplinary-evil approach in our response to these issues. Because such approaches can cause more harm to those who are affected or those who are the victims. For example, in communal riots always some are victims and some are the culprits.

Again, the state of Kerala witnessed an unprecedented flood which spread havoc in several districts in 2018. Several people lost their loved ones and livestock. The Kerala government sought the help of the Indian Navy and Air Force. Efforts were made for evacuation of those who were afflicted. But the swift response of a group of fisher men from Kollam and Alleppy deserves special mention. On their fibre boats they saved over 65,000 people according to government reports. This is almost double than those evacuated by the military helicopters! In their rescue mission one fisher folk even made his back available for people, especially the old ones who were in the floods to enter into the boat! Another aspect to be noted is the spontaneous response of our youth from different religious traditions. They used their smart phones smartly; without any particular leadership, they were actively involved in the rescue operation and afterwards for the cleaning work along with the government agencies. All these are signs of hope in our times.

Now there is a growing awareness that the present pandemic crisis is mainly two-fold: On the one hand, it's a health crisis, on the other hand, it's an economic crisis. Only few nations in the world have addressed this two-fold nature of the crisis effectively. Those who thrive in the Neo-Liberal economic model are the investors, the technocrats, the Multi-National Corporations and so on. The COVID 19 is considered by many as an opportunity to re-visit our model of development, which gives penury and marginalization to millions of the poor. Even in United States; there was acute shortage of some of the cheap medicines like Paracetamol, Hydroxycloroquine and so on which are used for the treatment of COVID 19. It has been pointed out that the Pharmaceuticals in U.S are not interested in producing some of these cheap medicines as they won't fetch enough profit! Hence, the U.S had to import this from India on an emergency basis. Well, the pandemic brings to the fore several of the life and livelihood issues and it's as if the so-called Globalization is taking humanity to the brink of a disaster.

Besides the above, does the COVID pandemic teach us anything? Perhaps, a few lessons are the following:

One: Our life is inevitably in the community. No one is an Island and we are not on our own. It's not just my health that matters but the health and well-being of the community.

Two: All of us are interdependent. All our actions affect the life of others. In a joint statement of the G20 countries after a virtual meeting in the context of the COVID-19 pandemic, this insight is brought to the fore: "*The unprecedented COVID-19 pandemic is a powerful reminder of our interconnectedness and vulnerabilities. The virus respects no borders. Combating this pandemic calls for a transparent, robust, coordinated, large-scale and science-based global response in the spirit of solidarity.*"[3]

Three: In spite of all the developments in the field of science and technology, notwithstanding the contributions of them in the area of health and medical field, there are also threats to human life at different levels.

Four: Human finitude. Despite all the achievements of modern science and technology, human beings are limited, and science doesn't have answers to some of the ethical issues within its framework. Rajeev Bhargava sheds light on this paucity of modern science in his article "*Revisiting Scientific Temper*": How can modern science be valorised after an awareness of the devastation it has caused? Nuclear destruction, industrial pollution, climate change, and a technologically induced sedentary lifestyle are all undeniable facts."[4]

Five: Re-discovery of our family time. Some of our family counsellors have always been telling us to set apart quality family time. It seems, those exhortations almost fell on deaf ears as we were too busy with our work, business, and so on. Surprisingly, the Government of India declared March 22, Sunday as the 'People's Curfew Day' and all were challenged to stay at home! Now, we have come to our senses; and all are at home. Well, there are several creative things that we could do during this time to promote the quality our life such as reading, writing, cleaning, gardening, and so on. Since many in the IT field are working from home, parents were available to their children.

Six: There is spiritual life beyond ritualistic rigidity. The religious leaders are struggling hard to grapple with the reality of this crisis. In the Christian church traditions, the complete lockdown declared in India by the Prime Minister, is during the period of Lent. In spite of the loss of revenue to be collected during this period for several charity programmes of the church; it is commendable that the church leaders have welcomed the lockdown for the common good. This is not to say that we can glorify the social distancing that is advocated by the Health Department as a remedy for the pandemic onslaught, or that the church services are not necessary. Perhaps, one of the lessons here is that we can conduct our rituals and practices differently; and heavens won't fall down if such things are done. Now several of the churches have started virtual Communion services, Bible studies, and so on! But a word of caution is also necessary here: While giving due recognition to the Governments' Mandate to keep social distance in the context of the spread of the pandemic; let us not go with the message that we are on our own and the community life is dangerous and so on! Similarly, within the framework of the church; a casual and lethargic approach is possible: It is ok to be at home, don't bother about the wider family of God, or liturgical and community life and so on!

The need of the times is to promote signs of hope at different levels. As C. S. Song, the Taiwanese author writes so poignantly: *What we need is a strong faith in tomorrow despite the bitter disappointments of yesterday and the cruel realities of today.*[5] This is possible only through God who is always the source of life, love, and grace.

5. Promoting Signs of Hope

In a report of the Eminent Person's group constituted by the WCC to watch over the elections in South Africa, it says:

> "*We could see a spirit of reconciliation at work at this moment of liberation. There was a reverence about the voting, and for the people of all faiths, there was a sense of God's gracious presence in history healing, reconciling, and giving hope for the future.*"[6]

Afterwards, Bishop Desmond Tutu thanked God for the "incredible miracle of free elections!" There are similar signs of hope all over the world, within the church and outside. Let me close with a recent example: The first COVID-19 patients in Kerala were from Italy; who transmitted the disease inadvertently to the parents back home on arrival. They were treated at the Medical College in Kottayam, Kerala. The last to be discharged were, the aged parents, who were above 80's. After being discharged from the hospital, the entire medical team came out to bid them farewell! Afterwards, two nurses who treated them, after their period of quarantine informed the Health department of Kerala that, given a chance, they would prefer to go back and serve in the COVID-19 patients' ward!

In Paul's letter to Timothy, this dimension of collective hope is brought out:

> *As for me, the hour has come for me to be sacrificed; the time for me is here to leave this life. I have done my best in the race. I have run the full distance; and I have kept the faith. And now there is waiting for me the victory prize of being put right with God, which the Lord, the righteous judge will give me on that Day, and not only to me but to all those who wait with love for him to appear* (2 Tim. 4:6-8).

Paul's life of contentment and sense of hope in the context of the early Christian community are evident here. As N. T. Wright observes: "*If we want a mission-shaped church, what we need is a hope-shaped mission.*"[7] As mentioned earlier, it is not just my hope, but it is within a community of hope that my hope is also nourished.

This is very often considered as a holistic approach. In order to promote hope, we need biblical foundations as well as a passion for truth and justice in the community. In Christian ethics, there are two approaches in this regard. The first one is how can I be good and avoid the evil? The second approach is how can I be good and resist the evil? In order to resist an evil, first the source of that evil, the infrastructure of it, the method of operation, who all are affected, etc. are to be discerned. The need of the times is to promote hope at different levels. This is possible only through God who is always the source of life, love, and grace.

Conclusion

Both the Jewish and Christian eschatology emphasize the dawn of a New Age and hence our task is to see beyond and to reach out in hope. In other words, we must be able to discern the birth pangs or labour pain in our socio-political fields. This is definitely an active hope and not a wishful thinking or facile optimism. Hope is not a sedative Christian utopia! It begins and grows in our concrete life here on earth and its culmination is in the fullness of eternity. An African saying goes like this: "You cannot wipe the tears of others without having your hands wet!" The anchor of Christian hope is Jesus Christ and his cross and resurrection. He challenges us to face the harsh realities of life. Life is not always solving problems; sometimes it will be coping with them as our counsellors say, confronting them as they come, and leaving the outcome confidently in the hands of God.

The crucial questions to be asked are these: Can we as Christians share a common hope? Can we promote symbols of hope by attuning ourselves to the divine and also by immersing ourselves in human realities and historical predicaments? Is the world in which we live the world that we want to live? Is the church that we are a part of the church that we want to be? Yes, there is always a gap between the ideal and the actual. But we are historical human beings. Christian faith has both historical as well as trans-historical dimensions. Hence, a world-negation or escapism should not exist in our spiritual life. The prophets of the Old Testament were social critics and God's politicians. There is so much to do that we cannot afford to be people who are alien to the Biblical truth:

> *So we cannot lose heart. Even though our outer nature is wasting away, our inner nature is being renewed day by day. For this slight momentary affliction is preparing us for an eternal weight of glory beyond all measure, because we look not at what can be seen but at what cannot be seen; for what can be seen is temporary, but what cannot be seen is eternal* (2 Cor. 4:16-18).

What we need today is a fresh search for meaning and mystery of life, in the context of our historical ambiguities and predicaments.

In the preceding sections of this work, some attempts have been made to mark the contours of a revised eschatology vis-à-vis Christian Hope. Throughout this book, the eschatology of the end time enthusiasts and Biblical literalists has been challenged. This is not an attempt to make any shallow value judgments on any church tradition. Rather, this is mainly because of the divisiveness and the tragic ethical consequences they create within the community of faith. What we need to underscore is an eschatology that is historical, prophetic, and transformative in nature. It is to be remembered that God's will for us has to be fulfilled in our life; in the midst of its challenges, ambiguities and uncertainties.

The main focus has been that in Christian Eschatology, the future has already come in the person and work of Jesus Christ. He is the One who enables and challenges us to walk an extra mile, to see realities with new eyes, and to be with those who are in dire need of our presence. Therefore, what we need today is an eschatology that is down-to-earth, an eschatology this is centered on the crucifixion and resurrection of Jesus, an eschatology that would empower us in our journey of faith. As pointed out in the preceding sections of this book, it is to be reiterated that this approach is based on the life and mission of Jesus Christ in its entirety, not just on a few eschatological or apocalyptic references. Any attempt to construct an eschatology that is alienated from the life, experiences, aspirations, and struggles of the people would be against the mind of Christ.

As we have seen throughout this work, though human destiny has both historical as well as trans-historical dimensions, what is required of us is to take our life of faith seriously through meaningful choices in our life. Our life on earth is neither to be absolutized nor to be negated. We are all historical human beings and our obedience to God as concrete historical human beings is what makes our life of faith authentic.

What we need is an attitude to life that sustains and enriches relationships and hope in the community and also a pursuit of life that affirms and strengthens people in their journey of faith. That is why Paul could affirm with great conviction, "For I am sure that neither death nor life, nor angels, nor rulers, nor things present, nor things to come, nor powers, nor height, nor depth, nor anything else in all creation, will be able to separate us from the love of God in Christ Jesus our Lord" (Rom 8:38-39). We should remember that these words are from Paul, who is known as the suffering Apostle. He challenges us to see beyond the negative and destructive forces, because they don't have the final say within God's providence.

The Christian Church is called to be a sign and agent and witness of this hope in the world. What is to be underlined here is the rediscovery of our inner spiritual potentials. All followers of Christ are endowed with charisma or spiritual gifts. We have potentials and limitations within us. What is desirable is a constant review of our spiritual forces which are the gifts of the Holy Spirit.

As mentioned earlier, the need of the times in to reiterate the theme of the 8th Assembly of WCC, "Turn to God and Rejoice in Hope." This also suggests that our ultimate ground and anchor of hope is God who is always active in His creation. Here we also have to discern all other false assurances of hope such as naïve and otherworldly spirituality, Christian cults, and end-time prophets and their spiritual gimmicks! Let us be assured that God is the one who instils rays of hope in the midst of despair and hopelessness. This hope is for the whole world, not merely for Christians. The question is whether we are facilitators of this hope wherever we are. In the search and manifestation of this dimension of hope, all those who are allies of life can work together. In other words, as pointed out earlier, only through the creation of a community of hope, can we also live and grow in hope. In conclusion, let me quote a prayer from the Collects of the Uniting Church in Australia, which seems to focus on some of the above concerns of this book:

In the midst of hunger and war, we celebrate the promise of plenty and peace;
In the midst of oppression and tyranny, we celebrate the promise of service and freedom;
In the midst of doubt and despair, we celebrate the promise of faith and hope;
In the midst of fear and betrayal, we celebrate the promise of love and life;
In the midst of sin and decay, we celebrate the promise of salvation and renewal;
In the midst of death on every side, we celebrate the promise of the living Christ.

Bibliography & End Notes

2. The Place of Eschatology in Theology

1. Jurgen Moltmann, *Theology of Hope* (London: SCM Press, 1967), 16.
2. Dermot A. Lane, "Eschatology", *The New Dictionary of Theology* (Bangalore: TPS, 1993), 340-341.
3. N. T. Wright, *History and Eschatology* (Waco: Baylor University Press, 2019), 79-86.
4. S. J. Samartha, *The Hindu Response to the Unbound Christ* (Madras: CLS, 1974), 157.
5. S. J. Samartha, *Preparation for Dialogue* (Madras: CLS, 1974), 155.
6. Owen C. Thomas, *Introduction to Theology* (Delhi: ITL, 1989), 208-212.
7. Leonardo Boff, *Faith on the Edge*, Harper & Row Publishers, San Francisco, 1989, p. 154.
8. M. M. Thomas, *Towards a Theology of Contemporary Ecumenism* (Madras CLS, 1978), 68-69.
9. *The New Dictionary of Theology*, p. 335.
10. Ruben Alves, "On the Eating Habits of Science", *Faith and Science in an Unjust World: Report of the World Council of Churches' Conference on Faith, Science, and the Future* (Geneva, World Council of Churches, 1980), 43.

3. Eschatology and Biblical Hermeneutics

1. J. R. Chandran, "The Authority of the Bible for Christian Social Action", *Religion and Society*, Vol. XXI, March 1974, 22.
2. Christopher Duraisingh, "The Authority of the Bible in the Modern Period", *Indian Journal of Theology*, Vol. 33, 1974, 75.
3. *Faith and Order Paper*, WCC, No. 59, 1971, 18.
4. Hans George Gadamer, *Truth and Method* (New York: Seabury Press, 1976), 250.

5. Paulos Mar Gregorios, "Hermeneutics in India Today in the Light of World Debate", *Indian Journal of Theology*, Vol. 28, 1979, 185.
6. S. J. Samartha, *The Search for a New Hermeneutics in Asia* (Bangalore: Board of Theological Education, 1987), 18.
7. Martin McNamara, "Inspiration", *The New Dictionary of Theology* (Bangalore: TPI, 1993), 524.
8. Clovodis Boff, "Hermeneutics: Constitution of Theological Pertinency", Vpoices from the Margin, R. S. Sugirtharahah (Ed.), Orbis, 1991, p. 30.
9. Smyth-Florentin Francoise, "A Christian Understanding of Fundamentalism", Religious Fundamentalism, John S. Augustine (Ed.), (Bangalore: SATHRI, 1993), 56.

4. What does the "End" mean?

1. Jurgen Moltmann, *The Coming of God: Christian Eschatology* (Minneapolis: Fortress Press, 2004), 216.
2. Abraham Heschel, *God in Search of Man* (New York: Farraf, Strau and Giroux, 1955), 19.
3. Kalinga Tudor Silva, "Beyond Social Distancing to Fight COVID-19", *The Hindu*, April1, 2020.

5. Apocalyptic Writings: Daniel and Revelation

1. N. T. Wright, *History and Eschatology* (Waco: Baylor University Press, 2019), 151.
2. "Commentary on Daniel", *Encyclopedia of the Bible* (Thiruvalla: TLC, 2006), 394-396.
3. For details see the author's book in Malayalam on Christology: *The Person and work of Christ* (Thiruvalla: TLC, 2017).
4. David Joy, *Kartrukahakalm Dhwanikumbol* (Thiruvalla: TLC, 2016), 11-19. (As the trumpet of the Lord sounds) Malayalam Commentary on Revelation.
5. Zoroastrianism, Wikipedia
6. Hans Kung, *Eternal Life?* (Eugene: Wipf Publishers, 1984).
7. Ania Loomba, *Colonialism/Postcolonialism* (Lindon: Routledge, 1998), 2.
8. Kwok Pui-Lan, "Gender, Colonialism & the Study of Religion", *Postcolonialism, Feminism & Religious Discourse* (London: Routledge, 2002), 15.
9. M. M. Thomas, *Christian Response to the Asian Revolution* (London: SCM Press, 1968), 22.
10. *Order of Holy Baptism*, Mar Thoma Church, 147.

11. Pablo Richard, *The Idols of Death and the God of Life* (Maryknoll: Orbis, 1983), 23.
12. Tom Driver, "The Case for pluralism", *The Myth of Christian Ùniqueness: Towards a Pluralistic Theology of Religions*, John Hick and P. F. Knitter, (Ed.) (New York: Orbis, 1987), 215.
13. Luna L. Dingayam, "Towards a Christology of Struggle: A Proposal for Understanding Christ", *CTC Bulletin*. Vol. X, No.1 (April 1991), 30.
14. Bertil E. Gartner and Gerhard Krodel, "The Lordship of Christ in the N.T.", *Christian Hope and the Lordship of Christ*, Martin J. Heinecken, (Ed.) (Minnesota: Augsburg Publishing House, 1969), 8.
15. Barbara R. Rossing, *The Rapture Exposed* (New York: Basic Books, 2004),109.
16. Chung Hyun Kyung, "Who is Jesus for Asian Women", *Asian Faces of Jesus*, Sugitharajah (Ed.) (Maryknoll: Orbis, 1993), 227-228.
17. Karl Marx and Friedrich Engels, *On Religion* (Moscow: Progress Publishers, 1975), 111.
18. Hans-Ruedi Weber, *The Way of the Lamb* (Geneva, World Council of Churches, 1988), 20.

6. Kingdom of God

1. Emilio Castro, *Sent Free: Mission and Unity in the Perspective of the Kingdom* (Geneva: World Council of Churches, 1985), 77.
2. Ibid., 51.
3. S. Kappen, Jesus Today, AICUF Publication, Madras, 1985, p. 11.
4. Leonardo Boff, *Jesus the Liberator: A Critical Christology for Our Time* (Maryknoll: Orbis, 1978), 60.
5. C. S. Song, *Jesus and the Reign of God* (Minneapolis: Fortress Press, 1993), 7-8.
6. Castro, op.cit., 69.
7. S. J. Samartha, *One Christ: Many Religions* (New York: Orbit, 1991), 170.
8. Paul Lakeland, "The Mission of the Church", *Constructive Theology*, Serene Jonesand Paul Lakeland (Eds.) (Minneapolis: Fortress Press, 2005), 234.
9. Raymond Fung, "Evangelism today: Sinners and sinned-againstness", *Asian: Christian Theology Emerging Themes*, D. J. Elwood (ed.) (Philadelphia: Westminister, 1989), 203.
10. *Springs of Living Water* (Geneva: WCC Publication, 2005).

7. The Day of the Lord and the Son of Man

1. *Dictionary of Biblical Theology* (Bangalore: TPL, 1967), 110.
2. William Barclay, *The Gospel of Luke* (Philadelpia: Westminster John Knox Press, 2001), 257.

3. *Dictionary…, op.cit.*, 112.
4. *Dictionary…, op.cit.*, 562.
5. Rudolf Bultmann, *Gnosticis Redeemer Myth*, Wikipedia.

8. The Cross and Resurrection of Jesus Christ

1. Kazav Kitamori, "Theology of the pain of God", *Asian Expressions of Christian Commitment*, T. Dayanandan Francis and Franklin Balasundaram (Eds.) (Madras: CLS,1992), 226-227.
2. Emilio Castro, op.cit., 73.
3. Jose Cardenas Pallares, *A Poor Man Called Jesus* (Indore: Satprakashan, 1986), 96.
4. Ibid., 130.
5. Deshmond Tutu, God has a dream, p. 107.
6. Article by the author "God in Your Grace Transform the World", *Messenger*, 2005. A publication of the Mar Thoma Diocese of North America & Europe.
7. Allan Boseak,Walking on Thorns; The call to Christian obedience,W.C.C, Geneva, 1987, 60.
8. S. J. Samartha, *The Pilgrim Christ* (Delhi: Asian Trading Corporation, 1994), 63.

9. The Ascension and Return of Jesus Christ

1. Jurgen Moltmann, *The Coming of God: Christian Eschatology* (Minneapolis: Fortress Press, 2004), 26.
2. Deshmond Tutu, op.cit, p. 107.
3. N. T. Wright, Surprised by Hope (New York: HarperCollins, 2008), 142.

10. Millenarianism, Messianism, and Rapture

1. Moltmann, op.cit.,192.
2. Dermot A. Lane, "Eschatology", *The New Dictionary of Theology* (Bangalore: TPS, 1993), 333.
3. Moltmann, op.cit., 147.
4. Reza Azlan, Zealot: The Life and Times of Jesus of Nazareth, Harper, 2013, p. xxiv.
5. C. S. Song, *Third-Eye Theology* (New York: Orbis, 1990), 258.
6. Barbara R. Rossing, *Rapture Exposed* (New York: Basic Books, 2007), vii.

11. Eternal Life

1. Paul Tillich, *Sytematic Theology* (Chicago: University of Chicago Press, 1973), 397f.

2. Katherine Wagner, *Life in an Amish Society* (Lucent Books, 2009), 28-29.
3. *Springs of Living Water* (Geneva: WCC, 2005).

12. New Heaven and New Earth

1. Ibid., 404.
2. Leonardo Boff, *Faith on the Edge* (San Francisco: Harper & Row Publishers, 1989), 158.
3. Wright, *Surprised by Hope, op.cit.*, 122.
4. Samuel Rayan, Anger of God, op.cit., p. 1).
5. Moltmann, *op.cit.*, 295.
6. Philip Woods, *People's Reporter*, January 2020.
7. Aruna Jnanadason, "God in Your Grace Transform the Earth", *Green Gospel* (Publication of C.S.I Synod Ecological Committee, 2010), 26.

13. Last Judgment

1. Wright, *Surprised by Hope*, op.cit., 117.
2. Owen C. Thomas, *Introduction to Theology*, op.cit., 213.
3. Samuel Rayan, *The Anger of God* (Mumbai: BUILD, 1981), 10.
4. Hans-Ruedi Weber, *The Way of the Lamb* (Geneva: WCC, 1988), 29.
5. Moltmann, op.cit., 255.
6. M. Shawn Copeland, "Human being", *Constructive Theology Classical Themes*, (New York: Fortress Press, 2005), 80.
7. Jesudas Athyal (Ed.), *Mission in the Market Place* (Thiruvalla: CSS, 2002), 37.

14. Graceful Living, Ageing and Dying

1. Nithya Chaithanya Yathi, Daivam Satymo, Mythyayo? (Malayalam), Is God Myth or Real?, Current Books, Kottayam, 1987, 51-53.

2.S. Kappen, *Jesus Today*, op.cit., 30.

3. Copeland, op. cit., 97.
4. Ibid., 103.
5. "Continuing Expression of Hegemony", *People's Reporter*, February-March 2020, 1-5.
6. Ibid., 31.
7. *The New Dictionary of Theology*, op.cit, 333.
8. Boff, *Faith on the Edge*, op. cit.,152.
9. Samuel Rayan, "That the world might be saved", Clarence O. Mc Mullen (Ed.), *Death and Suffering in Indian Religions* (Bangalore: CISRS, 1983), 39.

10. *New Vision for a Changing World*, Ecumenical Publication in Malayalam, July 2008.
11. Unction is considered as one of the sacraments in the Eastern Church tradition. In the Mar Thoma church, the liturgy for Unction has two parts: The first part is for the healing of the patient and the second part for a graceful death.
12. Wright, *Surprised by Hope*, op.cit., 151.

15. Church as a Community of Hope

1. Mathai Zacharia, *Theology for Our Times* (Bangalore: E.C.C, 1996), 17.
2. C. S. Song, *Theology from the Womb of Asia* (Maryknoll: Orbis, 1986).
3. Hindu, March 26, 2020.
4. Hindu, March 18, 2020.
5. Song, op.cit., 216.
6. Report of the Eminent Person's Group, EPS (Geneva: WCC, 1994).
7. Wright, *Surprised by Hope*, op.cit., 194.